ID0412447

Compass Points: Building Your Story

A guide to structure and plot

Compass Points: Building Your Story

A guide to structure and plot

Kelly Lawrence

**COMPASS
BOOKS**

Winchester, UK
Washington, USA

First published by Compass Books, 2014
Compass Books is an imprint of John Hunt Publishing Ltd., Laurel House, Station Approach,
Alresford, Hants, SO24 9JH, UK
office1@jhpbooks.net
www.johnhuntpublishing.com
www.compass-books.net

For distributor details and how to order please visit the 'Ordering' section on our website.

Text copyright: Kelly Lawrence 2013

ISBN: 978 1 78279 608 4

All rights reserved. Except for brief quotations in critical articles or reviews, no part of this
book may be reproduced in any manner without prior written permission from the publishers.

The rights of Kelly Lawrence as author have been asserted in accordance with the Copyright,
Designs and Patents Act 1988.

A CIP catalogue record for this book is available from the British Library.

Design: Lee Nash

Printed and bound by CPI Group (UK) Ltd, Croydon, CR0 4YY

We operate a distinctive and ethical publishing philosophy in all
areas of our business, from our global network of authors to
production and worldwide distribution.

CONTENTS

For my mother, Danielle, for introducing me at a young age to the power of a good story.

Acknowledgments

Many thanks to all at Compass Books, particularly Suzanne Ruthven for her advice and encouragement.

For all the wonderful storytellers, known and unknown, who have inspired me over the years.

For my readers, especially all those who take the time to post reviews or drop me a line on Twitter. Writing can be a lonely business without this interaction.

For all writers who are currently wrestling with their latest piece of work to the point of despair... you are not alone. And it does get easier. Honest...

Introduction

No Structure, No Story

What exactly do we mean by talking about structure, and just why is it so important?

In the most basic terms if you don't have a structure, then you don't have a story. Structure and plot are sometimes used interchangeably, but although closely interlinked they are not quite the same thing. Your plot is what happens in your story; your structure is a map for how that plot unfolds. Think of a plot as the bricks of your novel, and structure as the cement that holds it all together, as well as the overall shape.

In effect then, the structure is the shape of your plot and the foundation of it. It holds your story together. Your structure is your guide for what happens when, and it shapes your plot into a coherent narrative. Without a well-structured plot it doesn't matter how beautifully you write or how wonderfully imaginative your original idea, you still don't have a story. What you have is a pile of writing. It may be genius level writing, but it isn't a story.

If you are the sort of writer who, rather than planning every plot detail meticulously, likes to take a good idea and run with it (which inevitably leads to far more editing later on) then having at least a basic plan in place before you begin ensures you won't stray too far away from the path and end up, a third of the way into a draft which started brilliantly, scratching your head and thinking 'now what?'

Of course, that's not to say that you can't alter your original structure. Or that you can't make changes as you go along to your initial plot ideas; on the contrary. Having a basic plan in place before you get down to the main writing will help you identify where and when changes can or even need to be made, and the implications these may have on the story as a whole.

The very word 'structure' itself can sound off-putting. It conjures up something rigid and fixed, as in the wall metaphor. It certainly doesn't sound very creative. Yet it is the very tightness of a well-structured plot that keeps a story moving forward. And your story should always be moving forward. Even during times of exposition or even backstory and flashback, the story should always be moving forward (more of this later). This is particularly true if you are writing for publication with the aim of producing a story with wide commercial appeal. In today's ever changing market and fast-paced society even best-selling romances and family sagas are often as pacy as a Dan Brown or James Patterson thriller.

Think of your structure then as the lines of a motorway, guiding your story vehicle forwards rather than letting it meander off to do some sightseeing along narrow country lanes.

Chapter Breakdown

It is of course up to you how you choose to read this book, whether you read it from cover to cover or dip in and out of the bits that seem most relevant to you, but I would advise that you do the writing exercises and 'mini-exercises' in the order given. Each chapter, although more or less self-contained, also follows logically on from the other, ending with an afterword that brings everything together and provides tips to help you structure any past, current or future projects; as well as suggestions for 'mini-exercises' scattered throughout the whole text. This is followed by an appendix of resources which includes a look at some of the new story writing software and asks if any of this can be helpful with the issues examined in this book.

Notice what I've just done there? Read the preceding paragraph again. It sums up the structure of a particular book – the one you're holding in your hands. Although a non-fiction work, it has a recognisable structure; an introduction followed by five chapters, each with their own mini-structure of sub-headings followed by writing exercises and a chapter summary; an afterword that sums up the message of the book, followed by an appendix. Sometimes, as we will see in the first chapter, it really is as simple as that.

Anyway, on with the chapter breakdown...

In the first chapter we're going to look a little more closely at the definitions of plot and structure and the relationship between them, as well as examples of structural and plotting techniques such as the basic three act structure and the oft repeated assertion that 'there are only seven plots in the whole world'. We will take an in-depth look at these before going on to look at more complex structural techniques, layered plots and some excellent contemporary examples of both. There are also exercises to help you construct a basic skeleton of your proposed novel and an introduction to the fantastic technique of mind-mapping, if you are not already familiar with this.

Novel and fiction writers can learn a lot by looking at the structure of screenwriting and the story lines of certain movies and I'll be taking an in-depth look at this in chapter two, along with further exercises and a look at the 'writer's journey' as described by Christopher Vogler. This is used extensively by screenwriters and has much to contribute to the novelist also.

In chapter three we'll examine the importance of pace in your novel, what this means and how a tightly structured plot is essential. As well as a look at continuity issues (a common gripe from editors) the chapter focuses on introducing conflict into your story and adding tension in order to keep your story engaging and moving forward, as well as taking an in-depth look at the use of time.

Chapter four deals with the drama – the high points and turning points of your story that come about as a result of the conflicts – and we will see how these are enhanced by a tight structure and powerful plot, including the importance of establishing setting and building up to the high moments, how to effectively foreshadow dramatic turns, and craft a successful resolution or impact.

The fifth chapter covers external and internal journeys within your story and your main characters experiences and how these should mirror and support each other. We will begin to bring everything together in this chapter to demonstrate how a simple initial structured plan can be built upon to produce a richly layered, thoroughly engaging story that keeps the reader turning the pages.

I'll end with a look at how you can identify structural issues that may be present in a current or past project and how to use everything we've just learned to rectify them. It's my aim that by the end of this book you will have a more in-depth understanding of the process of constructing your story. An appendix takes a look at recent software that can help with the planning process.

These are issues that affect all writers, I believe, at some point or another, including myself, so this is also very much a distillation of everything I have learned and am still learning. Writing, after all, is a journey.

Exercise – Recognising Structure

Get a notebook (you may wish to purchase one specifically for the exercises in this book) and three of your favourite or most read works of fiction (perhaps even include a narrative non-fiction such as memoir, biography or travel writing if these are genres you are interested in). Try to choose three works that are very different in style, tone and genre.

Flick through and make notes on how each novel or book is structured. If you're not sure where to start, ask yourself the following questions about each one.

Is there a defined beginning, middle and end?

Is the novel divided into parts and chapters and can you see an inherent structure in how this has been done? For example, a story told by two different narrators might have alternate chapters in the different voices.

Is the story linear? In other words, does it go from A to B or does it move backwards and forwards in time? What time period does it cover; a week, a year, a century, and is this made explicit? For example many novels, particularly thrillers, often use the time period of the story as the very structure of their novel. A chapter for each day of the week, for example, with the day as the chapter title.

Who is telling the story? If more than one person, how is this done? Perhaps the story switches between first and third person, for example.

Make notes on the above and anything else you can think of, and then compare all three stories and see what similarities and differences you notice. Do you think the structure of any of these works affected your enjoyment of them?

Put your notes away to come back to later; we'll be using them again in Chapters One and Two.

Introduction Summary

- 'Structure' refers to the overall shape of your story, as well as the means by which your plot is crafted into a coherent narrative.
- A strong structure and tight plot, rather than forcing the writer into a rigid formula, in fact keeps your story moving forward and makes it easier to see where changes are required.
- These are highly important elements if you wish to write a story with strong commercial appeal.
- Without a defining structure, you don't have a story.

In the first chapter, we'll go on to look at different structural frameworks and plot lines that have been employed by many bestselling authors and how you can use them in your own work, as well as looking at contemporary examples of more complex plotting and exercises to help you begin planning your novel – or re-structuring an existing one.

Chapter One

Structural Techniques
and Crafting your Plot

As I mentioned before, the words 'structure' and 'plot' are used so interchangeably and so often in discussions of story crafting that they can come to mean the same thing, or even mean very little. In this chapter then I'm going to briefly strip things down to the bare bones before looking at more complex aspects of plotting and structure.

According to the Oxford English Dictionary, these are the definitions of the words 'plot' and 'structure' as refers to story-telling:

> *Plot* – 'the main events of a play, novel, film or similar work, devised and presented by the writer as an interrelated sequence'.
> *Structure* – 'the arrangements of and relations between the parts or elements'.

The Three-Act Structure

The typical story narrative is divided into three parts; beginning, middle and end. Sounds easy enough, although many writers struggle to divide their major plot points up between the three acts and end up with that well-known and dreaded phenomenon of a 'saggy middle'. This occurs when everything happens in the beginning and end of the narrative and not a lot goes on in the middle of the story. Having a well thought out synopsis and/or chapter breakdown beforehand helps guard against this happening, as does using Aristotle's interpretation of the three act structure.

Rather than dubbing it simply 'beginning, middle and end'

Aristotle termed the three acts 'set-up, conflict and resolution'. This immediately dubs the 'middle' of the narrative as the place where most of the story unfolds, and structuring your story in this way can be a big help in unfolding your plot in a way which ensures your story never loses momentum.

Thriller novels – naturally full of conflict – are often excellent examples of well set up three act structures, as well as genre romance novels, which are often written to fit a certain formula. To take my first in a series of Renaissance romance novels for Harlequin Mills and Boon, 'Borgia Fever' as an example, I deliberately used Aristotle's simple but effective structure to help my plot unfold. Although it required more forward planning than I was previously a fan of I found my story flowing effortlessly once I had a basic plan to follow, and my editor was both pleased and surprised to find it needed virtually no alteration.

If you are interested in a more in-depth look at this deceptively simple way of planning your story, I look at Aristotle's three acts in more depth, along with a detailed step-by-step writing exercise, in my guide 'Passionate Plots' (Compass Books, March 2014).

As I mentioned earlier, to many writers the idea of mapping out your story beforehand may feel alien and overly formulaic if you are typically a 'seat of your pants' kind of writer, but it really does make the whole process more streamlined and without necessarily compromising on creativity. The trick, as with so many things in life, is not to go to extremes, as the following two examples illustrate.

In many of her interviews and non-fiction novels, acclaimed author and writing coach Natalie Goldberg has confessed that writing her novel 'Banana Rose' was the hardest thing she's ever done, mainly because she launched herself into the first chapter without any forward planning whatsoever. After both friends and editors described it as beautifully written but completely plotless, it took Goldberg an incredible six years to whip Banana

Rose into a publishable novel. Which just goes to show; no structure, no story. At some point this work needs to be done, and it's generally more efficient to get your structure and plot in shape beforehand than to spend months or even years on revisions and rewrites.

At the other extreme, an editor of crime fiction once told me a story about a submission she had for a contemporary thriller. The author described – in pages of detail – how he had read all the bestselling thriller novels he could find and drawn up a graph of all the similarities so as to map out the 'perfect plot' and then applied it to his own novel. The result? A generic, rigid, formulaic story that didn't capture the reader or lead them to care about the characters or the outcome.

So how much planning should you do? It will obviously vary from writer to writer – or story to story – but the bare minimum I would recommend is a brief synopsis of the plot and a breakdown of the structure as described in the first writing exercise when you looked at your favourite books. To give an example, here is the plan I used for the writing of 'Borgia Fever'.

Setting – Santa Maria Palazzo, Rome
Timeframe – Over the course of one night, from a ball to the next morning. Year 1501
Chapters – Five, roughly equal length
Tense – Third-person
Viewpoint – Third person, but switches between Bella's viewpoint in chapters one, three and five, and Marco's in chapters two and four.

I followed this with a brief synopsis/chapter breakdown covering the main plot points, bearing Aristotle's framework in mind to ensure the first chapter effectively set up the story which then unfolded through the three middle chapters – no saggy middle in sight! – and was resolved with all conflicts and loose ends tied up into a satisfying ending in the final chapter. The synopsis doesn't have to be pages long either – mine consisted of bullet points. Just make sure you get down the main events and turning points.

Many writers do prefer a more detailed plan, especially if writing a more complex story, and certainly when you get to the stage of submitting your work you will be required to produce a more detailed synopsis, but this is fine as a starting point. I think of this as a 'skeleton structure'.

Exercise – Skeleton Structure

Take a story you have in mind, one you are currently working on, and one you have previously written (that remains unpublished) and write out a 'skeleton structure' for each as described above. If you like you can also – or alternatively, though I would recommend you include at least one of your own stories – do this for the three books you made notes on in the last exercise. Compare the three, and in particular take note of the following:

- When working with a previously written story, writing a skeleton structure should be very easy. If it isn't and you find yourself getting confused, it's a sign this work has structural issues. By applying a skeleton structure to it you may be able to rework it and even resubmit.

- When working with your idea for a future story, see how devising a skeleton helps you plan it more effectively. Contrary to the idea that structure and planning implies a rigid approach, many writers find that giving their work this kind of detailed attention gets those creative juices flowing.

The Eight Point Arc

The above three act structure and skeleton synopsis is one of the most basic ways to plan and plot your story. A slightly more detailed but still simple method of structuring your plot is the eight point arc, described in great detail by author Nigel Watts and expanded on by screenwriting expert Christopher Vogler in his work on mythic structure for writers (which we will look at in the next chapter). This story arc can also help you set up your three acts and can easily be incorporated into the simple synopsis in the above exercise. The eight point arc pinpoints eight main plot points that will be present in most of the classic seven plots (see below). The eight points consist of:

1. Stasis. The very beginning, before anything actually happens. Harry Potter's dreary existence at the Dursley's for example. In a contemporary novel, as little story time should be given as possible to this. In fact many authors will start with step 2 and then weave the necessary background in as they go along.
2. Trigger. The event or conflict that starts everything off. To stay with the Harry Potter example, a mysterious letter arrives...
3. Journey. The trigger starts the main character/s off on some kind of journey, be it an inner transformation, a fantasy quest or a race against time to dismantle a bomb. Or Harry Potter going off to Hogwarts.
4. Conflicts/complications/obstacles. The main body of your story starts to form, and this will take up the main part of your plot. The main character faces a series of challenges or surprises on their way to the end of the story. Harry settles in at Hogwarts, makes friends and enemies, tries out for the Quidditch team, survives attempts on his life, and starts to piece together the mystery of the Philosopher's Stone.
5. Choice. Some kind of critical choice has to be made which determines the ultimate outcome and also often reveals the true nature of the main character. Harry chooses to

saves his friends and go on to face the incarnation of the evil Voldemort alone...

6. Climax. The highest point of tension in your story. Harry battles Voldemort to the death.

7. Reversal. The outcome of the Choice and the Climax. Some kind of reversal occurs – generally a positive one for the main character. Harry defeats Voldemort and is healed of his grief for his parents somewhat when he realises his mother's love saved him.

8. Resolution. A return to stasis, although it will be a different state to the one we began with. Harry returns home to the Dursley's for the summer holidays, but he is a changed boy with his newly awakened wizard powers.

As I discuss in 'Passionate Plots' the stasis, reversal and resolution segments should be no longer than necessary. Start and end as close to the trigger and climax as possible, particularly with a contemporary romance or thriller.

The eight point arc would fit into the three act structure as follows

Set up
• Stasis
• Trigger

Conflict
• Journey
• Obstacles
• Choice

Resolution
• Climax
• Reversal
• Resolution

Mini Exercise – With this in mind, choose one of your skeleton structures from the above exercise and incorporate the eight point arc into your chapter breakdown.

Complex Structures

As well as being 'divided' into three acts and eight plot points, the typical story narrative will unfold in a linear manner. This may unfold naturally, with the plot simply going from beginning to end without overt mention of the time frame in which the story unfolds, or the time frame may be used as part of the structure – as in the seven day example mentioned in the Introduction. Not all stories however unfold in a linear manner but may move backwards and forwards in time, perhaps ending at the same point at which it began (a circular narrative) or even weave different stories together which unfold in different ways. Nevertheless, the overall arc will still fit the basic structures used in your 'skeletons' albeit in a more complex way.

A story can also be made more nuanced by using different voices – the two main characters for example, or even a group of characters. Jodi Picoult, author of 'My Sister's Keeper' to name just one of her bestsellers, often switches between a third person narration (he said, she said) and the voice of one or more of the central characters (I said).

Although more complex structures can be used to great effect, they are by nature more difficult to write and even more difficult to make work. If you are a new writer or are writing in an entirely new genre then it may be good advice to stick with a simple structure. Simple is often the most effective. Nevertheless, some stories lend themselves particularly well to a more complex set-up, and the structure itself becomes part of the story. A recent and award winning example of a highly complex structure is Gillian Flynn's 'Gone Girl' – arguably the best literary *and* commercial thriller of 2013.

'Gone Girl'

Gone Girl by Gillian Flynn was hailed as a literary masterpiece as well as becoming a mass market bestseller. It can be rare for a book to rise to the top of both the literary and commercial markets, and as well as Flynn's evocative writing and the fact that the work is a typically gripping, pacy thriller, the way the novel was structured undoubtedly played a big part in its success. The book is written from the first tense viewpoint of the two main characters, Nick and Amy, who are husband and wife. The premise of the book and the reason for the title is Amy's sudden and shocking disappearance on the eve of their wedding anniversary.

In the first half of the book, Amy is missing. Nick's chapters (they take an alternate chapter each) follow a linear narrative from the day of Amy's disappearance onwards, covering a period of a week, reflected in the chapter headings. Amy's chapters on the other hand take the form of her diary and go right back to the beginnings of the relationship up to just before her disappearance. This discoherence in the time period of the narrative voices is crucial to the plot twist that comes in part two of the novel, when Amy's narrative comes up to the present day, though remains a few days behind Nick's, and ceases to be in diary form. The structure of this story then, both in terms of time and viewpoint, is deliberately complex and nuanced.

On top of all this the author employs an 'unreliable narrator' viewpoint in the first half; meaning that 'diary Amy' is almost unrecognisable as 'real Amy' (I'm trying not to give too much away here). The result is really quite stunning. Although 'Gone Girl' came in for its fair share of criticism (as indeed do most runaway successes) mainly because neither of the main characters are particularly likeable and for the ending, which some found anti-climactic, others chilling, nevertheless lovers and haters alike admired the way she had shaped the narrative. Although this is an excellent example of a more complicated structure, bear in mind that it only works so well because the way the story is shaped is integral to the unfolding of the plot and its many twists and turns. If 'Gone Girl' was simply written in a linear fashion without the unreliable narrator element and the two 'voices' then the impact of the story's central twist would have been significantly weakened. In fact, the story simply would not have worked, reading like a second-rate generic thriller at best (although Flynn's elegant prose and punchy dialogue may arguably have saved it). The message? Only use a complex or non-linear structure when the story calls for it. Don't take a perfectly good story and play around with it unnecessarily. When in doubt, A to B is not just the safest option; it's usually the best.

Still, it's always worth familiarising yourself with more complex works of fiction, particularly as your own writing progresses and your critical faculties sharpen. My own recommended reading list, as well as Gone Girl, would be as follows:

Stephen King – The Shining (jumps around in time and features the 'voice' of a building!)

Irvine Welsh – Trainspotting (jumps around in time, is written from the viewpoint of various characters, and in different tones of Scottish dialect. Not easy reading, but incredibly powerful.)

Alice Sebold – The Lovely Bones (narrated by a murdered girl, moving in and out of her 'alive' viewpoint and the more dispassionate voice of her disembodied spirit. Eerie.)

Mini Exercise – Have a read of these and similar books and you'll soon see that the very concept of structure actually offers incredible scope for creative planning.

The Seven Plots

There is a well-known saying, expanded on in a recent guide by Christopher Booker, that when it comes to story-telling, 'there are only seven plots in the world'. That applies not just to novels but all forms of storytelling from ancient myths to the intricate worlds of online gaming. Humans are story-telling creatures and, it is believed, these basic frameworks are embedded so deep in our collective unconscious we often even unknowingly attempt to shape events to fit them. Whatever the truth of that, we can certainly see them playing out in our written work. The seven plots are generally described as:

- Confrontation – where the protagonist must overcome the adversary or disembodied threat to their way of life. Think Beowulf, or 'Star Wars' or Harry's struggle against Voldemort.
- Rags to Riches – where the protagonist loses something only to gain it back in a better form, which also helps them grow as a person. Many romances that start with a break-up follow this format. Also of course Cinderella, and even Bridget Jones.
- Quest – where the protagonist goes off on a journey, symbolic or otherwise, ultimately achieving or finding something that both saves and changes them. There are a wealth of stories, both classic and contemporary, that use this framework, from 'Watership Down' to the 'Da Vinci Code'.
- Voyage and Return – similar to the quest, except it plays out in a more circular manner, and the protagonist returns back to where they started. Think 'Alice in Wonderland' or 'The Lion, The Witch and the Wardrobe.'
- Comedy – where the protagonist is prevented from achieving their goal by often humorous obstacles, but it all comes right in the end. Modern romantic comedies are the perfect example of the modern use of this plot form. A classic would of course be Shakespeare's 'A Midsummer Night's Dream' or 'As You Like It'.
- Tragedy – where the protagonist suffers some downfall, resulting in his or her demise. Almost a reversal of the 'rags to riches' tale. 'Macbeth' and 'Dorian Gray' are typical

examples. This plot form tends to be less popular than it once was apart from in horror novels, although Irvine Welsh's 'Filth' is a quirky and powerful example.

- Redemption – where the protagonist starts off being rather unlikable or even downright evil but events transpire that causes them to redeem themselves over the course of the story. The Lestat character in Anne Rice's Vampire saga achieves this to dramatic effect over the course of the series.

Mini Exercise – You will find that nearly any story you read, watch or hear will follow one of these basic plots. Try grabbing a few of your favourites, along with some new tales in an unfamiliar genre, and see if you can identify which of the seven plot forms they are based on.

Not all writing and literature experts agree with the delineation of the classic seven plots however. Harry Bingham, author of 'How to Write' argues that all of the above can be distilled down into two – the Classic Plot or the Mystery Plot, and adds another – the Literary Plot, which is any novel that follows its own rules and attempts to break out of the traditional plot definitions. Scarlett Thomas, the bestselling author of 'The End of Mr Y' adds another plot in her work on literature 'Monkeys with Typewriters' as well as redefining and modernising others. Her classic eight plots are:

- Tragedy
- Comedy
- Rags to riches
- Quest
- Coming of Age
- Stranger comes to town
- Mystery
- Modern realism

Mini Exercise – If you're interested in plot definitions I would recommend any of these author's works for further exploration. The point I want to stress here is that, regardless of which 'plot' your own current work or idea falls into, it will be how you structure it that determines its impact. Take any example of any of the plots outlined above, particularly a work you have already looked at as part of the exercises in this chapter, and a close examination will reveal you can most likely break it down into the three acts and eight points. Have a closer look and see if you can identify the structural elements that help the plot unfold.

Plot and Structure – Bricks and Mortar

To go back to my initial 'building' analogy, let's take a closer look at how plot and structure can intertwine. As shown in the example of 'Gone Girl' certain types of plots can be showcased more effectively according to the way they are structured. With the earlier example of the thriller set over a period of seven days, the tight structure gives the sense of impending catastrophe and racing against time that makes a thriller, well, thrilling.

We've looked at the 'seven plots' (or three or six, or eight, depending on who you listen to) and the eight point arc that provides a map of how each may unfold, but another plot consideration that affects the choice of structure and vice versa is the element of story that dominates the narrative. For example, people often talk about a plot being either 'character' based or 'action' based. These are the most typical distinctions, but there are also two other elements may that determine the shape of your story; a 'world' based plot and an 'idea' based plot. I'd like to take a look at each of these in turn and how the over-riding theme of your plot ties in with the chosen structure of your narrative. We'll begin with the two most common, typical of commercial novels; character and action.

Character – All stories have characters, of course, and even in a more action based tale we need well drawn main characters that we can relate to and empathise with – even root for in their darkest moments. With a character based plot however this is taken one step further and the over-riding theme of the story is not so much what the character does but how they are transformed by it. Whatever actually happens in the tale is secondary to the inner journey that the character/s go through. This type of plot may be expected to be found in family sagas or romances but in fact is just as common in more action packed novels – the horrors of Stephen King are sometimes heavily character based; *Misery*, for example.

The paranormal crime *Anita Blake* series written by Laurell K Hamilton is also heavily character based. Each book is tightly plotted and packed with murders, werewolf wars, preternatural love triangles and the like, yet the overarching theme of the whole series and each individual book is the profound transformations – not always positive – Anita experiences as a result. The tortured inner wrestling with her emotions and eventual triumph over her inner demons makes Hamilton's bestselling series stand apart in a market saturated with paranormal stories.

Structuring of a character based story is in effect quite simple; it begins at the point when things begin to change for the character, and ends when the inner journey is complete. They are often, although not always, told in the first person. There can be variety within this; if the plot focuses on two main characters then they may take alternate chapters or a half of the story each; flashbacks and flash forwards may be used; perhaps the story, a la Bridget Jones, is told in diary form; but nevertheless that character arc remains the over-riding structure.

Action – In an action based plot the characters don't actually take a back seat as such (otherwise the reader is likely to discard the story out of sheer disinterest in what happens to any of them) but nevertheless it is the events that take centre stage. Or more accurately, one particular event starts off the action, and the story only ends when the consequences of this are resolved.

Andy McNab's war and espionage novels are good examples of this, but an action based plot doesn't necessarily mean a thriller; J K Rowling's *A Casual Vacancy* is a small-town story with a myriad of richly drawn characters that is undoubtedly action/event based. The story begins when a local councillor dies and leaves his seat open. Cue a spiralling sequence of events that drag all of the characters in, only reaching a climax when the seat is filled.

Action based plots are often tightly structured within a short, linear time frame to give the feeling of events spiralling. A myriad of viewpoints often works, but so can just one or two. To use the above examples; Andy McNab often writes in one first person viewpoint (he famously started off his writing career with his own memoirs) whereas J K Rowling uses the third person viewpoint for nearly every character in the book (and there are many). Both work.

World – Also referred to as 'milieu' this is often the dominant story element in many fantasy and science fiction novels, where the setting takes centre stage. Characters may be deep and events rich, but they only take place and interact within the context of the world. Fantasy, sci-fi and paranormal authors refer to this as 'world-building' and will often have detailed overviews of everything about the fantasy world, from geography to social customs, before putting a story plot together.

Excellent examples of world-building obviously include J R R Tolkien's Middle-Earth and Terry Pratchett's Discworld. The Discworld series of books are excellent examples of the world dominating the plot. Colourful characters abound and Pratchett's stories are full of action, yet the Discworld itself is so richly drawn it becomes the main character and main event all rolled into one. The effect is made sharper by Pratchett's witty and often caustic comparisons between the Discworld and the world we know.

Many different structural techniques can be found in these types of stories, and often even quite a loose structure may be used (the world itself providing the parameters of the story). Pratchett's Discworld novels are typically one long piece of writing with no chapters, split into myriad third person viewpoints and sections of omnipresent third person narration (not associated with a particular character; *It was a Monday*, for example) that gives an overview of Pratchett's universe. They are usually linear though; whereas other world based plots often make good use of time-slips and non-linear narratives.

World based stories that are more tightly structured tend to be those where the 'world' in question is alien to the central character. The story begins with the events that lead the character to enter the world, and ends when they return home. *The Wizard of Oz* is a classic example.

Historical novels are also occasionally dominantly world based; in my personal opinion, however, historical novels work best when the pre-modern setting is used as a backdrop to the main story, adding context to the events and the character's journeys.

Idea – The idea based story is also referred to as a theme based plot or a plot that hangs on a question; generally a 'what if?' The story ends when the question is answered or the idea or theme is fully explored in the context of the story. Alternative histories are good examples of question based plots. What if Hitler had won? What if the Spanish Armada had invaded England? And so on.

Most of Jodi Picoult's bestsellers, although they read like typical character or action based plots, are in fact based on a question (to hammer this home, her publishers have now started putting these questions explicitly on the covers, effectively drawing readers in). This question is kept in the mind of the reader throughout the book, often leading the reader to ask themselves 'what would I do in this situation?' and immediately empathise with the main character. Another author who employs this to great effect is Diane Chamberlain. Exploring issues such as organ donation, teen suicides and even mercy killings, issue based novels of this nature tend to be popular with book clubs.

John Grisham's *A Time To Kill*, although structured as an action packed legal thriller like the majority of his novels, could also be seen as an idea based plot, asking as it does some very heavy questions about racial and social justice.

How the idea is explored or how the theme unfolds will then determine the structure. Question based novels will often be linear and pacy, though some of Chamberlain's novels prove an exception to this, interweaving different narratives and time slips.

Structuring plot layers

A plot layer is not the same thing as a 'sub-plot'. A sub-plot involves secondary characters following their own story arc. Of course any sub-plot should impact upon the main plot in some way, whether overtly or subtly, or it risks being superfluous. If you have an idea for a sub-plot that starts to take up as much time as the main story then it's an indication it probably needs its own book.

A plot layer, on the other hand, involves your main protagonists, and adds depth to their main conflict or quest. In many commercial and contemporary novels authors make good use of plot layers to add richness to their tales and depth to their characters. James Patterson heaps lots of problems and conflicts onto one of his main protagonists, Alex Cross. As well as the murder mystery he is solving, Alex has his love life to contend with, the stresses of being a single father to three children, dissolving and changing friendships, and quite often an old adversary on his tale. You can't challenge your protagonist enough (though do give them a break from time to time so you don't thoroughly depress your reader!).

I'm mentioning this here – we'll come back to the issues of

conflict and weaving your story together in later chapters – for the following reason. When thinking about your structure and story arc, be sure to include your plot layers. Each layer – or problem for your protagonist – needs to have its own turning point, climax and point of resolution, preferably in a way that ties in with the main story. Don't leave any loose ends (unless of course, you're planning a series, but even then it's advisable to leave things resolved *for now*).

Exercise – Mind Mapping your Plot

I've tried to give you in this chapter an overview of basic plotting and structural techniques, as well as a more in-depth look at certain aspects of structure and plot that should hopefully help you in planning your personal masterpiece. It may feel however, like quite a lot of information. Although I would always advocate planning over not planning, it is possible (as in the case of the would be crime author with his meticulously charted submission) to plan too much. Keep these frameworks in mind, as they are tools to help you, but remember that the most important, central aspect of any novel is that first flash of insight when you conceive of your story idea, whether you start with a character, event or setting. The trick is to take that initial nugget of gold and build it into a narrative, using some of the tried and tested techniques offered here.

An excellent tool for keeping all your initial insights and attempts to craft them into a workable plan is mind-mapping. This is basically a more advanced form of the typical brain-storming spider diagram or word webs you probably used at school. It's quite fun to do, but has also been proven to be an invaluable resource in universities, business organisations, workshops and, yes, for writers.

Mind-mapping was initial conceived by learning and memory expert Tony Buzan as a revision and planning aid for students, and has since been recognised as a versatile tool that uses both 'sides' of our brains to marry logic and creativity – exactly what a writer needs to do to construct a story. As it's also quite good fun, it will please those writers who cringe at the very word 'planning'. Here's a rough guide for how to do it for an initial plot structure, and you can find an excellent video demonstration at http://writetodone.com/how-to-use-a-genius-tool-for-writers-mind-maps/#more-605. There's also software designed for those who would prefer a digital version to pens (or, as we shall see, crayons) which I will look at in the Appendix.

Take a large sheet of paper – at least A3 and pens, pencils, or crayons. Buzan himself recommends the use of colour, as this gets your creative impulses firing. Don't just use colour indiscriminately however, but keep it consistent i.e. purple for setting, yellow for character, etc.

Draw a large circle in the middle of the paper and write your initial story idea, or the title if you have it. Then draw branches coming out of this with a word on each branch; setting, timeframe, viewpoint, characters, conflict, etc. You then use each branch to jot down your ideas for your structure and plot, adding a new branch for each new idea. Use words or phrases – even pictures or stickers if you will remember their meaning – rather than sentences. This way of planning often stimulates your creativity and you might find ideas coming thick and fast, even breaking through 'blocks' or offering solutions to tricky parts of your initial plot ideas. Don't censor yourself or worry about being 'messy' – you can if you wish draw up a completed mind-map later to use as a visual point of reference.

The beauty of mind-maps is that you can record on one page virtually a whole synopsis that in a linear form would take pages to write. They're an excellent tool both to provide you with a visual starting point for sitting down to write, and as a way to stimulate ideas and overcome 'blocks'. They also effectively illustrate just how creative a 'structure' can be!

Chapter Summary

- The three-act structure is a simple and effective way to begin structuring your plot and can help avoid a 'saggy middle'.
- Effective planning provides a balance between 'flying by the seat of your pants' and overly formulaic writing.
- Use the exercise given to construct a basic 'skeleton structure' taking into account setting, time, viewpoint, etc. and a simple plot breakdown.
- The classic eight point arc framework can help you break down your plot into a coherent narrative and can be applied to most tales, regardless of genre.
- Complex structures can work to maximise the impact of certain plotlines – 'Gone Girl' is an excellent example.
- All stories can be distilled down into classic plot frameworks such as 'tragedy' 'comedy' or 'mystery'.
- The four main narrative elements are 'character' 'action' 'world' or 'idea'. The element which dominates your story can help you decide on an effective structure.
- Plot layers also need to be worked into your overall structure, as well as having a narrative arc themselves.
- Mind-mapping is an excellent tool for creative planning and can be an effective resource for writers who dislike planning or who tend to over-plan, as well as being a proven tool to stimulate creativity and overcome 'blocks'.

I've covered quite a lot of structural techniques in this chapter, but these have mostly been applied to novels. In the next chapter I'll be taking a look at what writers can learn from movie plots and the work of screenwriting experts, as well as examining how structure affects the impact of a story when it is adapted from novel to film.

Chapter Two

Learning from the Movies

Ah, the Silver Screen. Hollywood and the world of film may be immediately more synonymous with dazzling special effects and beautifully Botoxed stars, yet movies can teach us a lot about structure, especially when viewed in comparison with novels; even more so when we see a film adaptation of a particular novel.

Screenplays, just like books, follow a plot arc and a structure and in fact often follow classic plot formats and the eight point arc even more closely than novels. A movie, after all, has around only two hours to tell a story, relying on visuals and dialogue rather than narrative, and so screenwriters must follow a tight plan. There's no room for lengthy descriptions or exposition such as we may find in a novel.

As there are such differences between them then, how can a writer of story rather than screenplay find anything useful in an analysis of the latter? Well, for two main reasons.

Firstly, as mentioned above, many bestselling novels become adapted for the screen. By looking at the way a story is adapted we get a lesson in how structure moulds content and how by changing the way a narrative is presented, it can also affect the way it is perceived. It's the perfect visual demonstration of some of the points about structure that I made in Chapter One.

Secondly, as I also mentioned above, many screenplays follow a plot line similar to those explored in the last chapter, and Christopher Vogler expanded on this in rich detail in his acclaimed work on screenplay writing, 'Mythic Structure for Writers', which has proved invaluable for many novelists also. We'll have a look at Vogler's mythic structure later in this chapter. Firstly I'd like to explore my first point by taking a closer look at a story recently adapted from novel to film; David Mitchell's 'Cloud Atlas'.

'Cloud Atlas' – From Novel to Film

'Cloud Atlas' was nominated for the Man Booker Prize in 2004 and has a very unusual overall structure, consisting of six separate stories that could all easily standalone as novellas in their own right. Mitchell weaves them together both with the implicit connections between them and the way in which he presents them. The first half of the book presents the first half of five of the stories, going forward in time. The stories start with a Victorian naval adventure all the way through to an imagined dystopian future set in Korea. In the middle of the book we then have the whole and complete sixth story, set in a faraway post-apocalyptic future. The second half of the book gives us the second half of the first five stories, but in reverse order; so we start with the Korean dystopia and end with the finale of the first story, set in Victorian times. Its circular timeframe and intricate structure won the admiration of critics and readers alike.

'Cloud Atlas' is an ambitious novel, both in terms of its scope and its structure, but Mitchell pulls it off both with his elegant writing and the subtle connections he makes between the stories. There are suggestions of reincarnation; a diary gets passed along to the next story, or an earlier character pops up; albeit much older. Primarily though this is very much an 'idea' based plot (or collection of plots) dealing with themes of social justice and the exploitation of the poor by the rich. The intricate structure illustrates these themes well.

But what about the film? It would be hard to imagine a movie that followed the initial structure of Mitchell's novel without completely baffling the watcher or causing them to simply lose interest. So the film directors didn't try, but instead went for a completely different format.

The movie, by contrast, rapidly cuts between all six of the

stories for the entire duration – nearly three hours – of the film. Perhaps to avoid overloading the watcher with too much rapidly changing sensory detail, the stories are much more similar in terms of pace and style than in the original novel. This perhaps loses some of the impact of Mitchell's evocative settings, but makes for a more pacy film.

It also alters the overall impact of the tale a little. The inter-cutting between the six stories that we see in the movie allows the connections between them to be made more explicit; crucial in a movie where we rely on visuals rather than the narrative description of a novel. The subtle suggestion of reincarnation is made explicit in the film, and the echoes of exploitation brought brutally to life.

A person who had only read the book, compared to another who had only seen the film, would therefore take perhaps very different perceptions of 'Cloud Atlas' away, even though the plotlines are changed very little. The difference in structure largely accounts for this.

Exercise – From Page to Screen

If you haven't already, read 'Cloud Atlas'. Then watch the movie. What impact do the differences in structure have on your experience of both? Do you think the scriptwriters could have done it differently? Brainstorm your own ideas on how the movie adaptation could have been done without straying too far from the basic plotlines.

Now take a novel that hasn't yet had a movie adaptation made. Try and choose one with a complex or different from usual structure. Try 'Gone Girl' as we've already looked at this in some detail. Read your chosen book if you haven't already; then think about how it could appear on the screen. What structural changes could be made, and how would this affect the impact of the story? If you already have experience of screenwriting, or would just like to try it, have a go at writing one of the pivotal scenes.

If you have a finished novel or detailed synopsis of your own, do the same with this. I personally love this exercise; as well as giving you the chance to look at your story from a different angle, you have a valid excuse for imagining the A-list elite in the role of your own characters!

In fact, many novelists who also love film and/or are visual creatures may find plotting becomes easier if they try visualising their story unfolding, scene by scene.

Vogler's Journey

Christopher Vogler is widely recognised as an expert on story structure. His ground breaking work, fully entitled 'The Writer's Journey; Mythic Structure for Writers' has become definitive reading for both screenwriters, students of both film studies and mythic structure, and novelists alike.

The book was born, believe it or not, out of a memo, circulated by Vogler while working at Disney Studios. The memo concerned Joseph Campbell's work on the hero's journey within various world mythological cycles, and the ways in which Vogler saw this 'hero's journey' playing out in the structure of on-screen stories. Vogler's ideas caused quite a stir, and were the basis for the eventual book, which is now translated into eight languages.

Vogler himself has since worked as a consultant for various Hollywood studios, and helped advise on blockbuster movies such as Fight Club, The Lion King and Black Swan. In his latest course 'The Essence of Storytelling' Vogler discusses how the use of powerful story structure grounded in myth can turn a film from merely 'mindless amusement' to conscious story-telling that triggers powerful emotions in the viewer, resulting in a 'healthy catharsis' (first described by Aristotle when discussing the impact of the Greek tragedy plays upon their audience). Powerful stuff.

Although aimed at screenwriters and moviemakers, Vogler's work is also enduringly popular with novelists. After all, story is story. The best novels, too, follow a similar structure and result in a 'healthy catharsis' on the part of the reader.

So what does this 'mythic journey' consist of? Vogler's structure is similar to the eight point arc we looked at in the previous chapter, though rather more expanded; progressing through twelve stages based upon Campbell's 'Hero's Journey'.

- Ordinary World – the beginning 'stasis'. We see our hero/ine in their everyday environment. To take 'The Lion King' as an example, we see Simba's world and his role within the pride and the 'Circle of Life'.
- Call to Adventure – the 'trigger'. The problem or challenge that sets our hero off on his journey. Simba is growing up and must prepare himself to be King.
- Refusal of the Call – any well-rounded protagonist is likely to have some initial debts about the problem facing them. A further push, either internal or external, is needed to send them on their way. Simba has no wish to grow up and be sensible.
- Arrival of the Mentor – this is usually where the mentor character steps in – someone who advises and urges on the hero at various stages in their journey – often when they are about to give up. Initially King Mufasa and then wise monkey Rafiki play this role for Simba in the Lion King. The mentor may often at first appear bizarre, annoying, or even an adversary until their true role becomes clear.
- Crossing the Threshold – the hero is off along their journey and overcomes the initial obstacle. Simba goes off into exile after his father Mufasa is killed by his brother Scar, which Simba thinks he himself has caused.
- Tests, Allies, Enemies – the conflicts and obstacles that will make up the majority of the 'second act'. Friends and foes appear, and the hero must overcome various setbacks and challenges.
- Inmost Cave – our hero is facing the ultimate ordeal and

takes some time out to reflect, or wrestle with their inner demons. This may be a dark time for the hero. Often the mentor figure will pop up to help them through.

- Ordeal – the hero faces his greatest fear, test or adversary. Things may seem hopeless. Simba gets up his courage to face Scar, only for Scar to reveal Simba's (unwitting) role in his father's death.
- Reward – in spite of the horror of the ordeal, the hero has managed to grasp some kind of token (physical or otherwise). In facing Scar and admitting his secret, Simba is finally in possession of his full courage and ready to become King.
- The Road Back – the final chase or confrontation. Simba vanquishes Scar.
- Resurrection – the hero, before he finally 'returns' or takes on his new role, must undergo a final redemption or transformation. Simba shows mercy to Scar (who then gets conveniently torn apart by hyenas) and takes his rightful place as King.
- Return – the hero is back, the reward has been achieved, and the ordinary world resumes, but with important changes. The rightful King has been restored and the Circle of Life is once again in balance.

Mini Exercise – With the above in mind, watch – or re-watch – Disney's most popular film The Lion King.

To help clarify how this fits in with the planning of your novel, Vogler's 12 steps fit into the basic three act structure as follows:

Set-up
- Ordinary World
- Call
- Refusal

- Mentor
- Crossing the First Threshold

Conflict
- Tests, Allies, Enemies
- Cave
- Ordeal
- Reward

Resolution
- Road Back
- Resurrection
- Return

The 12-steps also expand on our basic eight point arc as follows:

Stasis = Ordinary World
Trigger = Call
Journey = Refusal, Mentor and the First Threshold
Obstacles = Tests, Allies and Enemies
Choice = Inmost Cave
Climax = Ordeal and Reward
Reversal = Road Back and Resurrection
Resolution = Return

Mini Exercise – Take one of your synopses of your own work from the earlier exercise and incorporate Vogler's 12 steps. You can also add them to your mind-map from the exercise at the end of Chapter One.

Exercise – Going to the Movies

The first part of this exercise should be enjoyable! Get a stack of Hollywood blockbusters, including two films Vogler consulted on (which are less straightforward than The Lion King in their use of the twelve step structure, yet nevertheless incorporate it perfectly) like Fight Club and Black Swan. Get watching.

Choose your two favourites and draw up a twelve point story structure for each using Vogler's designations. Can you identify the different stages in your chosen films?

Now apply Vogler's twelve steps to one of the novels you examined in the first exercise from the Introduction. Then apply it to a work of your own.

Chapter Summary

- Movies are an excellent way to examine storytelling structure from a different angle.
- Examining the similarities and differences between a novel and its movie adaptation illustrates how a difference in structure can change our perception of the same story.
- Movies follow a story arc similar to that of novels.
- 'Cloud Atlas' is a contemporary example of how structural differences can make a movie adaptation seem very different to the original novel, even without making drastic plot changes.
- Try imaging how a movie of your favourite book, or even an example of your own work, would look. What structural differences might you need to make to adapt your story to the big screen?
- Try visualising your story unfolding scene by scene as you plan – this can be a powerful plotting technique.
- Remember; the same story can be told in many different ways. Structure is your main tool to help you do this.
- Christopher Vogler's work on mythic structure remains the definitive guide on structure for screenwriters and he has contributed to various blockbusting movies. Disney's The Lion King is an obvious example of the 'Hero's Journey'.

- Vogler's work on story structure has proved useful to writers of all kinds of story – novelists as much as screenwriters.
- Watch a few films and familiarise yourself with how they fit into Vogler's 'mythic structure'. Then apply this to some of the novels you have been working with.

It's time to come back to novels. Unlike films, they don't run over a set period of time and so it is up to the writer to determine both the pace of the narrative and the timeframe it unfolds in, which can be a powerful plotting device. We'll also look at that all important narrative element that will keep your reader turning the pages – tension.

Chapter Three

Run, Story, Run –
Pace and Narrative Flow

Pace

How fast or slow your narrative flows along is called its 'pace'. A typical assumption would be that a thriller would be very pacy, an emotional and complex family saga for example less so. Although often true, this is not necessarily the case. In general, contemporary novels of all forms are tending to become, in today's fast moving world, a great deal pacier. That doesn't mean you should attempt to 'rush through' your story to make it more commercially acceptable however, as this will often backfire. Generally the story will lend itself to a particular narrative flow, and the chosen structure can help reinforce this.

Writing style can make a narrative unfold at a quick or more leisurely pace; use of short snappy sentences and lots of dialogue will make the story unfold more quickly, while lengthy passages of description and exposition (a character's inner musings) will slow it down. A pacier novel will grip the reader, while a novel with a slower narrative style will absorb them into the story in another way.

A few popular authors known for having a 'pacy' style include:

- James Patterson (thriller)
- Karen Rose (crime)
- Penny Jordan (contemporary romance)
- Sherrilyn Kenyon (paranormal romance)
- Dean Koontz (horror)

Some popular authors who make more use of description and

exposition (to powerful effect):

- Stephen King (horror)
- Philippa Gregory (historical fiction)
- Karin Slaughter (crime)
- J.K.Rowling (fantasy, crime and contemporary fiction)
- Laurell K Hamilton (paranormal erotica/crime)

Mini Exercise – Choose an author from each of the above lists and read a sample of their work. Analyse how they use sentence structure, dialogue, setting and description to determine the pace of their narrative flow. Which do you prefer?

In terms of writing style, the following are indicators of different narrative approaches to pace:

A pacy novel will contain lots of

- Shorter sentences
- Crisp, punctuated dialogue
- Verbs – they are 'action' words, after all!

A less pacy novel will contain more

- Longer sentences
- Description
- Adjectives (but don't use more than one to describe any one quality)

As an example, the following could be a paragraph from a story with a fast pace:

He loved her. That was a given. But he'd be damned if he would let her walk all over him.

'I said no, Laura. And I meant it.'

Laura's eyes widened. She looked shocked, just for a second. Then her mouth curved into the seductive smile he knew so well.

'Are you sure about that Detective?'

She began to walk towards him.

The next paragraph says much the same thing as the preceding first two lines, but at a slower pace:

Although he loved her as deeply as ever, he had no intention of letting her play with his already tangled emotions, of letting her reel him in to her as she had done so many times before. Laura was dangerous, probably untrustworthy, and most certainly a distraction from the case at hand. Even now she smiled languorously at him, her body curved easily into her chair, eyes heavy-lidded with a practiced look of seduction.

'Laura,' he began, raising a hand to stop her when she attempted to cut in, no doubt in an attempt to dissuade him, 'the answer was no.'

Mini Exercise – Carry on with the above example – take the last three lines of the quicker approach and rewrite it to finish the more descriptive second paragraph.

There is nothing intrinsically good or bad about either approach. Don't fall into the trap of thinking a faster paced story is necessarily 'easier' to write than a more leisurely one. You will most likely naturally fall into one camp, an indication of your natural – and probably most effective – writing style.

The problem with writing in a more descriptive style is, of course, that you may simply bore the reader. The answer to this is to ensure that if you are writing three pages of description, it is because *the story calls for it*. Not because you want to show off your evocative writing style. In other words, it is somehow crucial to the unfolding of the plot, perhaps by providing a necessary image that adds to the feel of the story (Stephen King's eerie descriptions of setting for example) or by including information that foreshadows something to come. Every page – indeed every sentence – should count. Before we go on to look at ways of ensuring this is so, this is a good time to mention an issue that often comes up when thinking about narrative flow – continuity. Mistakes in continuity can jerk your reader out of the most page-turning story, causing your narrative to not just halt but go crashing into a brick wall.

Continuity

'Narrative continuity' is sometimes taken to mean a story that progresses forwards through time rather than jumping around – in other words, a linear structure – but in fact it is a bit more complex than that. Whatever the structure of your novel, continuity means that your story makes a *logical* progression from beginning to end. This is where we can best see the pitfalls of failing to structure a story well. If your tale jumps from scene to scene for no apparent reason, for example, or if it goes off on a tangent far away from the main plot – issues we discussed earlier on. Such issues are a common gripe for editors and can lead to your otherwise well written submission being rejected. Quite simply, serious continuity errors mean a great deal of editing. Yet another reason why having a basic structure in place is advisable before you get writing.

'Mistakes in continuity' can also refer to relatively simple mistakes that thankfully are easily rectifiable. Just as well as this tends to be another pet gripe for editors. Glaring inconsistencies in your manuscript can confuse and even annoy your reader. Common errors include:

- Inconsistencies of time. At the start of a scene, it's noon. Two pages later, when not a great deal has happened, the writer starts describing the night sky. To remedy this, make a note of the time, setting, etc in your chapter outline (which you have written, right?)

- Characters ages and names. This happens a great deal with minor characters. I do it myself. If you're not great with names/ages/descriptions make a list of your minor characters and keep it handy.
- Colours, clothes and objects. Seemingly insignificant details can suddenly become glaring holes in your manuscript if you keep making mistakes. One character's piercing blue eyes are a warm brown two chapters later, or a richly decorated lounge becomes minimalist, or a dress turns into a skirt...your reader will notice. They are building up a picture in their minds eye as they read and the information should stay the same throughout the story – this is what we mean by continuity.

A writer friend of mine summed it up, I thought, very succinctly; *the idea is to keep the information given to your reader consistent from beginning to end of the story so there is a smooth transition between chapters and scenes.*

To give you an example, my editor at Harlequin got very cross when, in my first historical romance, the heroine goes running off in only her underwear only for me to comment a few pages later that her blouse (that she hadn't had on but was now mysteriously wearing) was wet through. Thankfully the manuscript was still accepted, but bear in mind that more than one or two of these mistakes and it could well have ended up in the bin.

Of course, inconsistencies do slip by, sometimes not just past the author but past the editor, copy-editor and proof-reader too. A few famous examples include:

- Tolkien. Even this master story-teller made mistakes, for example in *The Lord of the Rings* Tom Bombadil is described as the eldest being in Middle-Earth. Later on it's Treebeard. The elves are referred to as the oldest race as well, but they do originally come from another world, so we can let him off on that one.

- Stephen King. In *The Green Mile*, Percy is described as lowering his hand as he speaks – even though he's trussed up in a straitjacket.
- Stephanie Meyers. In the final *Twilight* book, Bella hands her dad a plate with pancakes on. Two minutes later he magically finishes his bowl of cereal.
- Dan Brown. Silas in the *Da Vinci Code* is legally blind. Yet he accurately shoots a gun.
- J K Rowling proves that continuity has to reflect the realities of the outside world also. Dudley in *Harry Potter* throws his PlayStation out of the window – two years before they were invented.

Don't make the mistake of thinking that if Tolkien got away with it, you can. Tolkien got away with it *because he was Tolkien*. You and I are not. Besides which, if you make it to the top of the bestseller charts, do you really want to find your book featured on various blogs and websites where readers have great fun cataloguing all your mistakes?

We all make mistakes, of course, that's why even the best authors have their work copyedited and proofread. But you can guard against making obvious and potentially damaging ones by planning ahead and going through your manuscript with a fine toothed comb afterwards. Continuity errors will jerk your reader out of the story, no matter how hard you have worked on making it a gripping and pacy read.

Tension on Every Page

Regardless of how fast or slow your writing style, the reader will be kept gripped by one crucial ingredient of your story; tension.

Tension comes from conflict and the foreshadowing of it; from the tangled relationships between your characters and the 'will they, won't they' dilemmas. It is tension that keeps your reader reading until the end, not your witty dialogue or your beautiful description. Don't assume that a novel is pacy just because it has lots of short sentences and snappy dialogue either. If that dialogue consists of a chapter of camaraderie between characters and offers of tea and chats about the weather, then your narrative isn't just slow; it has stopped. The same applies to action scenes, believe it or not. If your story is action after action but some of these scenes in fact add little to the overall plot, then they're not pushing your story forward; they're causing it to meander off all over the place. A high level of tension will keep the reader gripped even if the novel is, at first glance, written to a much slower beat than your average thriller.

Karin Slaughter, a crime author whose name I included on the above list, writes with a slower narrative style than other contemporary crime authors, for example James Patterson, master of the page turner, and yet critics and readers alike have commented on the gripping nature of her novels. This is because they throb with tension; not a word is wasted.

Imbuing every page with tension doesn't mean your protagonist constantly needs to have a gun held to their head either. It can in fact be very subtle; the merest suggestion that something is to come. But it does need to be there. When Philippa Gregory in 'The Other Queen' spends two pages discussing Bess of Hardwick's concerns regarding her properties it isn't because the author likes to describe bricks and mortar. Rather it gives us a glimpse of the affluent property owner Bess becomes, and hints at the tensions in her marriage, as well as foreshadowing the fact that her castle will soon be a prison for Mary, Queen of Scots. Although the reader doesn't yet know exactly what's going to happen, glimpses are given that something will, and it involves Bess being a landowner, and being less than blissfully happy with her husband. Had this not been the case, it's likely that Gregory would have spent no more time discussing Bess's residence than was necessary to provide the setting.

Exercise – Adding Tension

Take a novel written by any contemporary author whose narrative style is considered less 'pacy' than others (use the list above if you're unsure). Find a section of description that is at least a page long. Can you find the tension? Try this again with any novel that you never finished because it was 'boring'. How much do you think a lack of tension may have contributed to your disappointment with it?

Now take your own work, preferably one you're in the middle of writing or editing. Find a page that is primarily description. Heighten the tension.

Now find a page that is primarily dialogue. Is there evidence of tension in this conversation between characters or are they simply passing the time of day? Heighten the tension.

Finally, go to a point in your story that comes just before a pivotal moment in the plot. Hopefully this will already be a point of high tension. Heighten it further.

Structure, pace and time

Whatever your writing style, your narrative will flow and keep the reader racing towards the end if you manage to hook them from beginning. Ask the story's big question at the beginning of the novel and answer it at the end – this creates a narrative line that will urge your reader on. Go back to the simple structures we looked at in Chapter One. That 'trigger' occurs in Act One, or the 'set-up' part of your story; not a hundred pages in. Get it on the first page, if you can. A structural device many novelists use to do just this is to make the first few pages of the novel a 'flash-forward' in time to that first call to action, then they come back to the necessary set-up and world-building (although I would recommend you weave this into your narrative as you progress through the first few chapters rather than making any one chapter or segment all about establishing background).

The time frame (or period) your story takes place in can provide a good 'peg' for your narrative and a basis for your overall structure. In some stories it *is* the structure – events unfold over a single action packed day for example, or the book explores a certain period of history or three generations of one fictional family. In such cases the sense of a certain amount of time unfolding helps determine the pace of the narrative. A five generational family saga is likely to feel less pacy than the story that takes place over a day, even if they have the same word count and are written in a similar style.

Yet even if you feel the notion of time is not a particularly important point in your story, it's still there in the background. Without time, your story can't unfold. So while you're plotting your story, ask yourself how long it takes to unfold, and how you could use this timeframe to shape your narrative.

Your characters experience of time can also provide you with structural ideas. If for example your two main characters have very different experiences of a particular event in time you may wish to include two different viewpoints in your novel, perhaps as alternate chapters. This device requires well-drawn and defined characters however who have something contrasting about the event to say – if their voices and experiences are similar your narrative pace will be in limbo.

Non-linear structures are currently popular and work well where there are secrets to be withheld and tangled relationships to explore. I've already given two extreme examples with 'Gone Girl' and 'Cloud Atlas', but another example are time slip novels – two or more inter-weaving linear narratives set in different time periods. Usually the 'past' story will reveal something that adds to the climax and resolution of the more current narrative. The critically acclaimed novels of Kate Mosse, Labyrinth,

Sepulchre and more recently Citadel are excellent examples of this structural device. This does however tend to make a novel feel less 'pacy'. After all, you're constantly going back in time! As always, the structure must fit your story. Dan Brown's 'Da Vinci Code' could hardly have been dubbed a thriller if he had employed an interweaving narrative that followed the original path of the Holy Grail around first-century Europe, for example.

Exercise – Playing with Time

Choose a character from the following list

- A postman/woman with a false leg courtesy of a war injury
- A seventeenth century Venetian 'lady of the night'
- A captured slave in 24th century Russia
- A police officer specialising in 'sniffer' dog handling
- A blind child about to start a new, mainstream school

Now choose – at random, maybe put them in a hat – an external conflict

- An unexploded bomb
- A midnight card game that turns murderous
- A murder of someone in power
- An earthquake
- The zombie apocalypse

Before you go to the final part of this exercise, briefly outline a story for the character and conflict you've chosen. It doesn't have to be more than a few bullet points.

Now – again at random – pick one of the following time frames:

- 12 hours
- A decade
- A ten day countdown…

- Three months
- A thousand years

Now think how you can apply this time frame to your story. How does it affect or further your plot? Can you structure the narrative around it? How does it affect the pace of your story?

Pick another timeframe (but keeping the same character and conflict) and repeat.

Chapter Summary

- The 'pace' of your narrative is how quickly your story seems to progress. Some commercial genres, for example, contemporary thrillers, demand a 'pacier' style.
- Writing style, sentence structure and the use of verbs or descriptive passages can influence whether your narrative flow is pacy or more leisurely.
- Both approaches have their advantages – and disadvantages – and suit particular stories. Read a variety of authors with different styles to get a feel for this.
- With more descriptive novels, passages of background setting, description and/or exposition should still move the story forward.
- Whatever the pace or style of a novel, it is the growing tension that drives the story and keeps the reader hooked.
- The best writers inject tension on every page; this can be very subtle, but it is there.
- Try the exercise to inject tension into your own narrative.
- You need to hook the reader from the beginning with the novels big question or challenge that then gets resolved at the end.
- This unfolds over a certain time period; and time can be a powerful structural device or hook.

- Different viewpoints of a certain event, non-linear structures, time-slip novels and countdowns are all ways time can be used to structure your novel.
- Try the exercise given to explore time as a structural device.

When thinking about the structure of your plot, it's likely you will have an idea of what the pivotal moments, or high points, are in your story. How these unfold are an important part of shaping your story – in one sense, your story is held up by these high points. Taking into account everything we've discussed so far, the next chapter looks at the dramatic turning points in your novel and how to set them up.

Chapter Four

Staging the Drama

Drama. That one little word means so many things, and these days it's often used in a negative way to mean 'too much emotional stress going on' or something like that. My nine year old daughter, in a recent argument involving two of her friends and a new toy, suddenly threw up her hands and announced 'I just can't deal with all this drama!'

We may try and avoid 'drama' in our real lives, but when it comes to our favourite stories, we crave it. All that lovely conflict and tension reaches boiling point and BOOM, something happens. Something that results in a plot twist, or even deeper conflict, or some inner wrestling for your main characters, up until we get to the climactic major drama near the end of your novel.

In other words, in a well-structured novel or story, the dramatic moments, or key points in your plot, will be tightly linked; each building on the one before it, escalating until we reach the climax and resolution.

In the last chapter we had a look at what may be termed the 'low points' of your plot, and the importance of filling them with tension. Now we'll take a look at the 'high points' or, the drama, and how in a well-crafted story the stage is set for them to occur at just the right time.

As I've mentioned before, and it really is impossible to stress this too much, something needs to happen as near the beginning as possible (the trigger in our eight point arc) so that your story begins at a high moment. As well as hooking the reader early on, this promises more to come. If we go back to Vogler's twelve step structure, we can see the high moments clearly.

- We begin with the ordinary world, which should hopefully be as brief as possible, or better yet woven in to the first few chapters which consist mostly of;
- The trigger, or call, which is our first dramatic moment, and the initial refusal of it, which adds to the sense of drama.
- We're introduced to the mentor, setting us up for the next dramatic moment of
- Crossing the threshold; this is likely to be a high point of the plot, even if the challenge is more an inner than outer struggle. Then we get into the meat of the story with
- Tests, allies and enemies. The main body of your story should have plenty of escalating dramatic moments, which serve to build up the story. Remember chapter three and the mention of continuity and logical progression?
- The cave often consists of a pause in the external action, building up the tension for
- The ordeal and reward stages, which are some of the key 'high moments' of the story. The drama should be coming thick and fast now, as we reach
- The road back. The final 'big drama' where it all turns around for our hero. After this highest point, the resurrection (which can also be very dramatic, particularly in terms of the inner conflict of the main character) and return should happen swiftly, leaving the story with a satisfying ending.

It all sounds simple enough, and yet many writers don't inject enough drama into their novels. That 'saggy middle' is often the main culprit, as discussed before. It's common for a writer to have a clear idea of the 'trigger' in their story, and of the climactic 'ordeal' and 'road back' stages, but only a vague idea of what's going on in the middle. As well as keeping the tension going from beginning to end as discussed in the last chapter, *things need to happen.*

If you look at a typical crime novel for example, where we start with an unexplained murder and end with it being solved, the story doesn't usually go from A to B without another murder, or the criminal stalking a potential victim that's close to the hero, or someone getting a severed finger in the post. If the whole story consisted of the hero simply going about their business solving the first murder with no other dramatic plot twists, we would have a pretty boring novel. The same goes for any other genre.

Take a romance novel. The hero and heroine don't just meet at the beginning and have a jolly nice time until they finally get it together at the end. Obstacles are constantly thrown in their way, until it looks as if their romance is never going to happen; leading up to some kind of showdown that in turn leads to a breakthrough in their relationship.

Again, it might seem obvious, but from talking to editors and agents, you would be amazed at how many manuscripts they see that get rejected simply because there is not enough drama; not enough high moments, not enough *stuff going on*. This nearly always occurs in the middle of the story.

Before we move onto an exercise to help with this issue, it's worth thinking about what 'drama' actually means. It can, but doesn't necessarily have to, refer to another body, or some terrible catastrophe, but may be more subtle than that. The high points of your novel can consist of:

- Moments of emotional breakthroughs between characters – forgiveness, break-ups and breakdowns, revealing of secrets, etc.
- Unexpected news (usually bad).
- One character making some sort of sacrifice for another or a higher cause.
- A reversal of fortune or someone changes their mind about a core issue.

- A main character faces a difficult moral choice.
- Someone close to the main character leaves town, turns out to have an ulterior motive, or dies.
- A pivotal erotic encounter.
- Something is achieved which is both important to the character and helps with the final showdown.
- A breakthrough in knowledge.
- An unexpected reunion.
- A face from the past reappears.

I could go on. The body of your story should contain at least some of these plot points. As long as the action spurs the story on, and makes sense in terms of the overall plot, then you really can't have enough drama.

Exercise – Where's the Body?

As I mentioned before, in a typical thriller/murder mystery, the drama escalates along with the body count. Your story may not warrant an actual dead body – it's a romantic comedy, for example – but if you find your story is flagging around the middle, or at any other point, chances are it needs your genre's equivalent. The following exercise was originally adapted from Donald Maass' 'Writing the Breakout Novel' and is a favourite of writers I have worked with.

Go through your current manuscript, or synopsis for your next project. Is there a character who could be forgiven by another? Make it happen in a touching, dramatic scene.

Is there the suggestion of a sacrifice on the part of one of your characters? Make this explicit in an emotional scene.

Does one of your characters face a difficult moral choice or change direction in some way? Make this the focus of a dramatic scene. Make the choice agonising. Torture your character a little.

In a story that *isn't a romance*, do you have two characters (one should be your main protagonist) who are attracted to each other? If so, ramp up the sexual tension between them and have it explode in an erotic encounter that has meaning for the plot. If you would like to explore this further, see my earlier writing guide 'Passionate Plots'.

If you are indeed writing a crime thriller, add another body. Make it a friend/sibling/ex-lover of a main character. Explore the implications for your overall plot.

If murder isn't appropriate, can you get away with killing off one of your characters? Or at least putting them in a life or death situation?

Do any of your characters have a secret? Reveal it in the most dramatic way possible. If they don't, give them one.

You might not want to keep all of these scenes in your story, but chances are at least two or three of them will add needed high moments to your plot.

Build-up and Impact

Your dramatic moments will be the ones that readers remember, but what's going on in between (remember that all important tension) determines the strength of the impact. Dramatic moments can't just be thrown in willy-nilly in an attempt to rescue a boring narrative, they need to both fit into and further your plot, and to make sense in terms of it. In other words, they don't just come out of nowhere. They are part of your plot. They're *structured*. Yes, that word again.

Quite simply, what is happening before the drama to lead up to it, and what happens afterwards; how does it impact upon your story and the characters?

Even if a particular high moment does seem to come out of nowhere to the main character, for example you're writing a twisty suspense thriller, and you want your reader to be shocked at where the story has just taken them, there still needs to be a precedent for it happening.

Let's go back to our 'where's the body' crime story, and let's say the second murder turns out to be the main characters long lost sister. There's a satisfying, dramatic plot twist that the reader won't see coming. However, prior to this scene you should have mentioned, or at least hinted at, the existence of this sibling. This actually makes the twist more shocking – as well as it making more sense – than if the reader had no prior knowledge. As well as looking as if you just chucked in a long lost sibling on a whim, the reader may feel cheated. It's far more satisfying to drop a few hints along the way, giving the reader that 'aha!' moment.

Of course, your high moment, or point of drama, may not involve a twist at all, but nevertheless there should be some kind of build-up to it, even if it is one that the reader only becomes aware of with hindsight – after all, you don't want your story to be too predictable. This build up to a dramatic event in your story is called *foreshadowing*. Typical foreshadowing techniques include:

- The characters themselves are concerned or apprehensive. If something's going to happen at a usually humdrum event, you can convey the fact that all isn't going to go to plan by making one of the characters nervous. The reader will pick up on this and expect that something is about to go down.

- Objects. Objects that later play a pivotal role in the story can be mentioned beforehand – use the 'rule of three' (we need on average to have something mentioned at three separate intervals before we pay attention to it). The reader might not consciously realise they're expecting that object to come into play, but when it does, awareness dawns ...'so *that*'s why'...

- Prior events. The most obvious technique to use; the events leading up to the drama unfold logically. This works for the type of drama that the reader is waiting for – the first kiss, for example – rather than an unexpected plot twist.

- Hunches and opinions. If the main character repeatedly confesses to a gut instinct that something isn't right, or has a seemingly irrational dislike of another character, you can bet that their hunch or opinion is going to be proved right. Or maybe even disastrously wrong. Either way, that opinion is being repeatedly voiced for a reason.
- Setting (we'll come back to this in more detail in the next section). If the writer makes much of the dark and stormy night, then something is going to happen in the shadows...

It's important to make sure you don't lead your reader unwittingly down the garden path. If you've got a mystery to reveal, you may want to place a few red herrings to keep your reader guessing, but do be careful that you don't do this unintentionally. For example, don't keep banging on about the beautifully carved walking cane that belongs to the villain unless it's going to be bashed around someone's head at some point or unscrewed to reveal a secret map, for example.

What about after the event? If you're at a midpoint in your story, chances are things aren't going to be resolved for a while, but nevertheless after each dramatic scene there has to be an impact. Something needs to have altered or intensified, paving the way for the build-up to the next major scene. To make sure your drama has an impact, ask yourself the following questions:

- How has the conflict or tension intensified?
- How has the mystery deepened, or has a new clue been uncovered?
- Have any of the relationships between major characters been altered?
- Are we any closer to answering the big question of the story?

For a high moment to be truly that, at least one of the above should apply as a result.

Establishing Setting

As mentioned above, the setting, both of your overall story and a particular scene, can give a hint of what's to come. It can even play a large role in determining your overall structure, depending on your plot and the genre. Think about the Harry Potter series for example, which is structured around the hidden-from-Muggle-eyes wizarding world in general and Hogwarts School of Witchcraft and Wizardry in particular. The series is structured around the school timetable, with a book per school year. Even in the final book, where Harry and co have prematurely left Hogwarts to go on their last dangerous quest, awareness of the school dominates and the friends eventually return for the final climactic showdown. Each individual book in the series is also structured around major events in the school year, with the high moments of the plot often occurring in tandem with a party, exam, or sports match. It's a powerful example of how the setting can provide a structural framework in itself.

Stephen King's 'The Shining' does a similar thing, albeit not so explicitly, with the Overlook, the haunted hotel in which the anti-hero slowly goes crazy. The ghosts and memories of the Overlook provide the basis for the non-linear narrative, with the Overlook itself even being included as a point of view character, as mentioned briefly in Chapter Two.

In 'Room' author Emma Donoghue goes a step further. The setting *is* the story; the tale of a young boy and his mother forced to live in one room by her kidnapper. The boy, Jack, has never known anything else and this one room is his whole world. This extraordinary use of setting makes for a tightly structured and powerful novel, if an understandably disturbing one.

Fantasy and science fiction novels, or indeed any 'world'

based story, will use setting as the ever present backdrop to all high moments in the story. Historical novels by their very nature make good use of both time and setting, as the plot unfolds in the context of the era.

But what if your story isn't 'world' based, and the setting isn't so integral to the plot, that as in the case of Hogwarts and the Overlook, it practically becomes a character in its own right? If your story is set in contemporary times, in a fairly typical modern city? Do you still need to worry about setting?

Yes, of course you do. Your story cannot exist in a bubble, it has to happen somewhere even if that *somewhere* is wholly fictional. Even if the overall setting plays little part in the plot, what about those high moments themselves? Here, setting can be incredibly powerful in terms of both setting the scene and giving the drama a 'stage' to play out on. Think Christian Grey's 'playroom' in 'Fifty Shades of Grey' where the drama of the heroine's sexual awakening largely unfolds.

Setting can either 'fit' the scene – as in the 'dark and stormy night' horror scenario, or be in such stark contrast to it that it actually intensifies the impact – evidence of a gory murder is found in a sterile hospital room, for example. Either way, give your drama a stage.

Establishing setting, however, doesn't mean pages or paragraphs of description – as we looked at in Chapter Three, this lowers tension and bores the reader. If you do feel you need a large chunk of description, ensure it foreshadows the drama in some way or adds to the sense of tension. Try not to overuse those adjectives either.

Mini Exercise – Contrary to what we're taught at school, you shouldn't use more than one adjective to describe the same thing, at least not unless you're describing different qualities, and even then there are better ways. Take the phrase 'dark and stormy night' that I've used above. I'm using it here to illustrate a point, but you wouldn't (hopefully) use it in your writing unless it was a deliberate parody. It's too much of a cliché. It would be more effective to just use 'dark' or 'stormy' or, if you really want to convey the fact that the night is both dark and stormy, try something like:

The sky was black, punctuated by the occasional zig-zag of lightning.

Find your own phrase to tell your reader 'it was a dark and stormy night'. Then re-write these phrases in a similar way:

The goose was big, fat and round.
the bright blue shiny engine
She was a happy, pretty little girl.

If you think these phrases sound childish, that's because I've taken them straight from my daughter's old Early Readers books. That's the effect of over-using adjectives in description – you will sound like your target reader is a five year old, no matter how complex your plot.

You can establish setting with a few choice descriptive sentences, preferably embedded in your narrative rather than a stand-alone paragraph, or you can do it more subtly. Try some of the following techniques:

- Use the five senses. Explore the setting through your characters' eyes – or ears, or nose…A well timed smell of engine oil will evoke the image of being in a mechanic's garage more strongly than if you meticulously described the interior.
- Through dialogue. Dialogue is a great way to show rather than tell. Have one character comment to another how rundown the neighbourhood is and how they would never

walk through it at night rather than spending half a page describing the street. If something is going to happen later on in that rundown street (and it should be, otherwise why is it getting a mention in your narrative?) then you've successfully foreshadowed the drama as well as providing the stage for it. Inner monologue and opinion can work in much the same way.

- Details through action. If you want to establish that your characters are in an overgrown garden, for example, have your hero impatiently brush away a tangle of weeds rather than describing every straggling tendril.

Sticking with the overgrown garden, look at these two paragraphs. The first is a block of largely unnecessary information. The second illustrates some of the techniques above.

They were standing in a large, unkempt garden. Weeds reached as high as their waists amid an overgrown lawn, dotted with dandelions. An old, rusted mower sat unused in a corner of the garden, leaning up against a crumbling brick wall. Opposite was a small shed, which was nearly covered with ivy and cobwebs, and an old clothes line snaked through the branches of overhead trees that blocked most of the sunlight.

I could go on. Maybe part of this description is significant – there's a body in the shed. But you wouldn't know it from reading this paragraph – there's nothing to suggest that the shed is any more interesting than the dandelions or the clothes line.

'Doesn't look as if anyone's been here for a while,' Mary commented, looking around at the unkempt garden.

John nodded, crushing weeds and god-knows-what-else underfoot as he walked over to a small potting shed and peered through the windows. He heard the greedy buzz of flies and held his breath. Through the cobwebs and dust, an all too familiar shape caught his eye.

'Mary. There's something – or someone – here.'

Mini Exercise – Have a go at rewriting the first paragraph yourself.

Author Joanne Reid has reportedly said it best, with the oft-repeated quote *'Setting should be like good wallpaper. It enhances your story, fits perfectly, and does not overwhelm the people in the room'*.

Exercise – Staging the Drama

Pick a setting randomly from the following list

- A tropical beach
- A train station
- A graveside
- New York
- A snowstorm
- A college classroom
- Your main character's kitchen

Write a few sentences to describe this setting, bearing in mind the above tips on the use of adjectives. Now randomly pick one of the following dramas

- A tearful goodbye
- An erotic encounter
- A grisly murder
- A family secret is revealed
- A marriage proposal
- Realisation of a new skill/talent that was previously unknown
- A plane crash

Briefly brainstorm a storyline or scene that marries the two. Now write the part *before* the drama, using some of the above techniques to both establish the setting and use it to foreshadow what's to come.

Chapter Summary

- A story needs drama, or high moments.
- Each dramatic event should be linked to the one before, giving a logical progression of events that leads up to the final climax and resolution.
- This needs to be kept up throughout the narrative, both to increase tension and avoid that dreaded 'saggy middle'.
- In crime novels, drama may consist of another body. But drama can mean lots of things, depending on your story. A kiss, a moment of redemption, a secret coming to light, etc.
- Try the writing exercise to add drama to a current story.
- The drama must further the plot, not just be thrown in to add interest.
- To make sense in terms of the plot, there must be some kind of build-up before the high moment, and an impact after.
- You can build up to or foreshadow a dramatic point in your plot in a variety of ways including through your characters, the setting, prior events or even symbolic objects.
- For your drama to have an impact on your plot, it needs to have effected a change or caused a heightening of tension and conflict.
- Setting can be used to set the stage for your drama, as well as being a structural device in itself.
- Establish setting through the use of dialogue, the five senses, short descriptive sentences and details revealed

through action, rather than overlong passages of information.

- If a detailed description is necessary for some later plot development, include only what is significant and try not to overuse adjectives.
- Try the writing exercise to explore how to establish setting and use it as a 'stage' for your dramatic scene.

In the next chapter we'll be looking at the overall story arc of both your external plot and your main character/s and how they should reflect each other to give your story both structure and depth. We'll also look at how to put together everything we've learned in order to create a well-structured, gripping narrative.

Chapter Five

Plot Mirrors;
External and Internal Journeys

Let's go back to Vogler's mythic journey for a moment. These twelve steps aren't just the outline of the external events, but illustrate the inner journey that the hero goes on as a result of them. As well as your overall story arc, your main character – or perhaps two, if you're writing a romance for example – follows their own, corresponding arc. Each dramatic event will have an impact on the protagonists' inner life. Each heightening of external conflict will enhance their inner struggle. This may not be as pronounced in an action based plot as a character based one, but it should still be there. Unless your protagonist is a robot.

To cite James Patterson again, his successful Alex Cross series are action led, fast-paced thrillers. Yet Alex's inner journey is never ignored. In 'Violets are Blue' for example, the plot is largely driven by the unfolding of a complex murder case involving serial-killing 'vampires'. There's also a sub-plot – resolved in this novel – carried on from earlier in the series where another as yet unknown serial killer is both stalking Alex and murdering his friends. Although Alex is swept up in this chain of events, never is he anything less than proactive. Neither is his inner development ignored. We see how the events affect him; more importantly, how they change him. We see the impact both on his love life and his relationship with his children. He doesn't just go back into a bubble at the end of each case to be brought back out at the beginning of the next – he has a richly drawn character arc.

Your hero/ine also needs their own motivations to be driving them; don't just have your character reacting to external events. Yes, they may be forced or cajoled into a certain course and have things along the way happen to them that are largely beyond their control, but nevertheless they have their own motivations and goals within this framework and can make choices with what they have, rather than mindlessly letting plot events determine their actions.

Look at the twelve step journey again and you will see that the mythical hero makes his presence felt. He is 'called' but at first resists rather than going with the flow. At some point he retreats into the 'cave' and has to face some tough choices, proceeding to the 'ordeal' through his own volition.

Mini Exercise – So when plotting your story arc, think also about the inner development arc of your main character. Make notes – perhaps do a corresponding plotline in a different colour – to show what is happening with your main character at each major plot point.

Motivation and Turning Points

As well as the external 'trigger' that sets your plot in motion, what inner motivation is driving your character forwards?

If you find this difficult to pin down, then ask yourself, *what are the stakes*? What does your character hold most dear. What is at risk for them? What do they want to gain, and what do they stand to lose? This is important, and ideally you should have the answers to these questions before you sit down to write. Yes, those characterisation exercises where you write down every detail about your characters from their first kiss to what they last had for dinner are useful; but the thing you need to know, and the reader most wants to know, is what is driving them?

In the above example, Alex Cross wants to solve the murders because of course, that's his job and innocent people are dying, but his ultimate motivation is keeping his family and friends safe. In the Harry Potter series, Harry may want to kill Voldemort partly because everyone keeps telling him it's his destiny, and if he doesn't then Voldemort will kill *him*, but his personal motivation is the fact that Voldemort killed his parents, and now he's threatening his friends. In the film influenced by Vogler, 'The Lion King', Simba has to kill Scar to take his rightful place as king, but this isn't really what's motivating him – rather it's the sense of shame he still feels about his father's death and his need for redemption.

Once you've determined your hero/ine's motivations and stakes, you can look at how these are affected by each turning point or dramatic event in your story and how this helps your character develop. Ideally, once defined these personal stakes should be raised right up to the final showdown, when your character hopefully achieves their ultimate goal. Either way, they should be transformed or redeemed in some way.

Along the way, events will test them, raise the stakes and cause some inner conflict. That's deep characterisation, and your reader will care more about your character's inner struggles than their star sign or the colour of their eyes. When your character develops along with your tense, dramatic plot, you have a powerful story.

Karin Slaughter does all of this very powerfully in her latest Will Trent crime story 'Criminal'. The story is tightly focused around a recently released serial killer who appears to be back to his old tricks. This external plot is tightly linked to the character development of both Will and his cantankerous boss Amanda. Using a time-slip structure Slaughter interweaves the past events, slowly revealing a secret in Amanda's past that affects Will in the present (one of the most powerful uses of time slip). Slaughter is a master at deep characterisation and creating characters that readers really care about, even when they may be pretty unlikeable people. She does this by making her characters intensely involved with the plot. Each case is, in one way or another, personal. In 'Criminal', Slaughter constantly raises the stakes for Will, until the reader is left wondering how he's managing to hold it all together and desperately rooting for him.

Exercise – Defining and Raising the Stakes

Take the main character of a previous, current or planned story, preferably one you've been working with throughout the reading of this book and in the previous exercises. Imagine you're having a dialogue with them just after the first external plot point has taken place – the 'trigger'. Put them in the 'hot seat' and ask them the following questions:

- What do you most want or need?
- What or who are you the most afraid of losing?
- Why are you doing this?
- What would be your preferred outcome?
- What would be the worst possible outcome for you?
- What is your greatest fear right now?
- What is your biggest dream right now?

Write down 'their' answers. Now ask yourself – what is their motivation, and what is at stake for them?

Once you've defined their stakes, you can raise them. Go to a point in your story that constitutes some kind of turning point for your character. Ask them the questions again. Now ask yourself – what could happen that will raise the stakes even further? If their motivation, like Alex Cross' is to keep their family safe, heighten the danger drastically. If they're desperate to confess their feelings to their long lost lover, have that lover move across the globe. Even if you don't want to do anything so drastic, or you can't fit it feasibly into your plot, you should be able to find a way to make your character's central problem *matter even more*.

Exposition

Exposition is the parts of your narrative where your character reveals their inner thoughts. Providing these are thoughts which illustrate their inner yearnings and conflicts rather than their to-do list or thoughts on décor, they can be powerful moments in your story. Nothing much is happening on the outside, but use exposition well and you can really up the tension levels in your story. Key moments of exposition also make your character's story arc explicit.

Using a first person point of view is ideal for exposition – indeed, as a first-person viewpoint indicates a character driven plot, exposition is essential to avoid that robot rearing its metal head. It also may seem easier, but the key here is to not overdo it, or give the reader long-winded passages that go off the point of the plot. The following paragraph shows how not to use exposition in the first person:

> *I was anxious and hungry so I made myself a sandwich. The cheese tasted delicious. It reminded me of that time Sheila and I went on holiday....*

Much more effective is something like:

> *I knew I needed to take a breather, to sit down and eat something. After the events of yesterday had kept me up all night, jumping at every noise, I hadn't been able to eat breakfast. The cheese was delicious, Sheila's favourite – oh God, Sheila – but I couldn't manage more than a few mouthfuls. I had always been like this; unable to eat when anxious. The product of growing up with my mother, perhaps.*

The second to last line shows us the real meaning of exposition – to reveal something of the character's *thoughts about themselves*. The first paragraph could have gone on talking about cheese and reminiscing about holidays for pages and would have told us nothing about the character's self-regard, thoughts about themselves or their circumstances and a knowledge of how life has shaped them. The second paragraph, if placed in the context of a plot, hints at all of these and can easily be expanded on. It's also more interesting.

It's just as easy to do in the third person, using a subjective rather than objective view – i.e. through the character's eyes rather than as a detached narrator. For example we can rewrite the second paragraph into the third person with much the same effect:

Heart racing, Mike knew he needed to take a breather, and that he should probably eat something. A sleepless night jumping at every noise had left his stomach churning and made breakfast impossible. He made a cheese sandwich and at the first taste instantly thought of Sheila. She had loved cheese. Mike pushed the plate away even though his stomach gnawed at him. The old anxiety was back, and with it the memory of his mother.

An anxious stomach and a cheese sandwich may not sound very dramatic or tense, but if it leads into a disturbing memory of his mother that then leads to a shocking realisation about 'Sheila', it turns out to be an effective tool for an inner turning point.

Exercise – Using Exposition

Take a look at the story you worked with in the previous exercise. After the scene where you've just raised the stakes for your character, give them some downtime to process recent events.

Using no more than one or two paragraphs, use exposition to explore how your character is currently feeling about their situation. Have your character, however briefly, reflect on themselves, their actions or their past. If you can, subtly hint at a conflict to come, reveal something not yet known to the reader about your character, or have your character come to an inner realisation.

Go back through this story if you have a completed or nearly completed draft, or back through any old – unpublished – work you have, and go to a point in the story where the character is mulling over events, having a bath, eating breakfast, etc. Are you making good use of exposition here, or is this passage just a 'filler'? If it's not doing very much, rewrite it using the tips above.

Have a look through a novel featuring a character you love. Find passages of exposition. Analyse them both for their effect on the plot and the character arc and also for how they help the reader empathise with the character. Think about the traits that make you identify with this character. Chances are these are at least partially revealed through exposition.

Using Structure to Weave it all Together

We've covered a lot of ground in this short guide. If you've been using it to help with a current story or story plan then you've hopefully done lots of work on tension, drama, setting and characterisation, as well as determining and strengthening both plot and structure. In a very real sense, structure is what holds all of these elements together. To keep things simple, let's look at how a simple three act linear structure provides both the overall shape for your novel and pulls everything together.

Let's say you're writing a historical thriller about a Nazi soldier who is in fact a spy for the Allied Forces. You've decided on a time frame of a year, a very specific year – the countdown to the end of the war (which our hero helps bring about). As this is a key element to the plot, you've decided on a chapter per month – so twelve chapters in all. Three for the first act, six for the second, three for the third. This very simple narrative structure will make it easier for you to plot your high points and key turning points and develop your character arc. You've even thrown in a romantic plot layer with a young Jewish woman who ends up helping our hero in some integral way.

Perhaps the best way to illustrate how having a framework in place would help you craft this story, let's imagine you hadn't. You just started with the basic idea of a story about a Nazi spy in the last days of the Second World War, and started writing, full of enthusiasm. Without the use of the three acts and a basic plot arc, your first three chapters wander around a bit covering background, characterisation and some dramatic war scenes that don't actually add much to our hero's journey. Finally our hero has his call to action and the story proper takes off. Halfway through it occurs to you a romantic element would be nice, so a chance meeting with the love interest pops up rather randomly. The story goes off on a tangent for a while exploring this before coming back to the main storyline. The romance and the spy elements therefore seem to have little to do with the other, making the romance merely distracting. Lack of planning means you go on for twenty chapters before realising the story needs to come to an end, which then occurs rather swiftly. Any sense of build-up – or countdown – has been lost. The tension ebbs and flows, rather than escalates throughout.

This is a fairly extreme example but nevertheless happens a great deal, particularly for first time novelists. I personally have five old half-finished drafts in my drawer – all abandoned due to lack of planning. Having a structural framework – however basic – to work within allows you to plot more effectively, heighten tension, work your inner journey into the external arc and ensure that drama is both logical and escalating. That doesn't mean you can't play around with it as you go.

Sometimes rules were made to be broken. In order to do that with any impact, they need to be defined in the first place.

Exercise – Putting it all Together

Take your current story, or one you've been working with as you've gone through these exercises. If you haven't already made a skeleton and/or mind-map for this story, do it now. Add in your chosen setting and timeframe, viewpoint you are writing in, and the 'big question' of your story.

Take your three acts, and divide your chapters up between

them. Work out where your eight –or twelve – major plot points are going. Make a few notes on what happens in each chapter.

Now for each chapter, make brief notes on how it opens, what the high moment, turning point or conflict/tension consists of, and how the chapter ends.

Do the same for each act.

Add in your protagonist's inner journey, plotting it alongside your external story arc.

Look back over this plan. Do you have enough detail to start writing your novel? If not, add as much detail as you need.

Now write your book.

Chapter Summary

- As well as your overall plot, your main character should go on an inner journey that reflects external events.
- Notice how Vogler's hero goes through stages of inner and personal conflict as he approaches the final resolution.
- Your character's inner journey is fuelled by their motivation, and pulled by their personal stakes in the matter.
- Use the exercise to define these stakes – and raise them.
- Each high moment of your plot should deepen your hero/ine's inner conflict or raise the stakes for them in some way.
- You can use exposition to illustrate what's going on in your character's head.
- The most powerful use of exposition deepens characterisation by revealing the character's *thoughts about themselves*.
- Make any exposition central to the plot.
- Having a basic structure helps you use these tools more effectively.

- **Use the final exercise to bring all of your notes together and create a detailed story plan.**
- **Write your story.**

You should now have a thorough understanding of plotting and structure and be able to start or continue your current project with a clearer understanding of these elements, resulting in what is hopefully a more powerful story. But what about older projects? Do you have a half completed or even completed draft of a story you absolutely loved that just lost its way somewhere? Or a manuscript that for reasons you can't fathom kept getting rejected? Or perhaps you've just completed a story and want to submit it but have a nagging feeling something isn't right?

Chances are the issues are structural, and if this is a project you believe in, it may be time for a re-write.

After the Draft;
Identifying Structural Issues

If you're having trouble deciding where the issues are in a particular manuscript, apply a structural plan to it such as we just used in the last exercise. If you can't effectively do that, this should flag up where the issues lie. For example, if you can't divide your novel into three distinct acts, you know you haven't defined your beginning and ending, in which case you probably haven't defined the trigger that sets events in motion, or resolved the big question – if there is one.

Luckily, structural problems are common and once identified, they can be fixed. Here are some typical structural issues; how to identify them and what you can do about them.

Issue – No 'big question'

Identified by – Your story is moulded around that 'big question' whether it be a will she/won't she dilemma, a mystery to solve or an over-riding theme about social justice. If this is lacking, it will affect the overall structure. There is no 'hook'. If your story seems to follow no logical course, or the resolution feels unfinished, or reading the manuscript leaves the reader feeling vaguely disinterested in spite of lots of drama and great characters, chances are you either haven't resolved your big question or failed to define one in the first place.

Strategies – Make or review a plan of your novel. Plot out your story arc as best you can. Now ask yourself, what is the big issue or key theme of this story? Most likely you will identify two or three possibilities that haven't been developed. Pick one. Decide whether this story is character or action based, or even world or idea based (in which case your core theme is absolutely key). A character based plot will have a big question that revolves around the main character/s. An action based plot's key issue will likely be more external. When you have pinpointed what the 'big question' is re-structure your story accordingly, ensuring each scene takes us closer along the path to resolving this key conflict.

Issue – That 'saggy middle'

Identified by – Around the midpoint of your story, the reader starts to feel bored, get confused or simply stops caring. The main events of the story happen near the beginning and the end. Open the story at random in the middle and you come across lots of 'filler' – description for the sake of it, meaningless dialogue, exposition that doesn't reveal anything profound... When you try and plot your story arc, you find that there's just not a great deal to say about the middle of the story and there are few key events.

Strategies – Use the three acts to define your beginning and ending. Now think about how you can use act two to deepen the conflicts that are present at the end of act one through the use of drama and tension. Apply Vogler's twelve steps and/or the eight point arc to your story to tighten it up. Have a big dramatic scene and an inner turning point occur around the midpoint of your story, and ensure personal stakes are raised. Introduce a new character/subplot/plot layer, providing it weaves into your plot and doesn't just arrive out of nowhere. If you're writing a suspense, plot a major twist here. Also – and this is difficult for many writers but often crucial – cut any superfluous descriptions, dialogue, interior monologues or events that don't further your plot. Every single one. Be ruthless. Often the middle of a good story sags because it's too long. Cut the parts that are dragging it down and you may find a well-structured novel emerges that requires little further work.

Issue – Lack of tension/conflict

Identified by – If this is present mainly in the middle of the story then see the issue of a 'saggy middle' above. If however your story in general is lacking in tension and conflict, then it needs a big injection of both at every stage. This applies to your manuscript if readers describe it as boring or it fails to hook them at the beginning. Look at your story premise. Is this a matter of life or death to the main character? Is there anything crucial at stake? If your answer is no, then you need to raise the game.

Strategies – Use the defining and raising stakes exercise in Chapter Five, and the adding tension exercise in Chapter Three. This may often be all you need. If you still feel something is lacking, add a countdown or race against time element. Ensure that all dramatic events are foreshadowed and have a discernible impact on both your plot and the main character's inner journey. Perhaps most crucially – look at the 'big question'. How much does it matter? If you're writing a romantic comedy, for example, finding the perfect wedding dress just isn't going to cut it. Planning the perfect wedding because the heroine has a point to prove to the ex she still loves (effectively changing the big question to 'will she get him back?') is better.

Issue – No defined time or place

Identified by – No time markers, and lack of clarity about how long a period of time this story covers. No identifiable setting, or setting is generic and clichéd and adds nothing to the story.

Strategies – Determine over what time period your story takes place. Is this or can this be made an element of the plot? If so, incorporate it into the structure for example with chapter breakdown and headings. If not essential to the plot your reader will still require a sense of time passing so embed this in your narrative with the odd – not too contrived – mention of a specific date (i.e. Easter) or a comment on how long has passed ('we had been together three months when he proposed') or even brief mentions of climate and weather to give a sense of time passing. Take a look at your setting and make notes about it. Refer back to the establishing setting section in Chapter Four and try the techniques listed there. Where are your major events taking place? Can the setting add to the impact? Again, refer to the exercise in Chapter Four.

Issue – Overly complex structure

Identified by – As well as a lack of structure a common mistake is for emerging novelists, eager for that bestseller, to use a too ambitious premise for the sake of showing off their skills and proving they are a 'serious writer' rather than because the story calls for it. Always, always, put the needs of your story first. Both readers and editors can tell if you're just trying to be smart and it quite often just won't work. Had Gillian Flynn used the structure for 'Gone Girl' on a straightforward thriller that didn't have such a startling midpoint twist and conflict between the major characters, it wouldn't have worked but just seem contrived. As it is it works because it was without doubt the *best way to tell the story*. Look at the novel version of 'Cloud Atlas'. If David Mitchell had been writing a generational saga in six parts for example, rather than a series of six stories set in different time periods and linked by the novels big ideas rather than by character or even plot, his unusual structure would have seemed odd and confusing. Look at your narrative with a critical eye. Does your story *need* to be told in this way?

Strategies – If the answer to the previous question is 'no' then ask yourself whether you want to rescue this manuscript because of its nifty structural technique or because you believe in the story. If you're driven by the story, break it down into a basic, linear plot arc and see if the story is still strong. If it is, tweak or rewrite as necessary.

Issue – Dissatisfying ending

Identified by – The ending feels anti-climactic. This is usually due to one of three reasons; the stakes weren't high enough, therefore the resolution had less impact; loose ends weren't satisfactorily tied up and questions – big or small – not satisfactorily answered; or the story goes on for too long after the final high moment.

Strategies – Raise the stakes and up the tension – again, see Chapters Three and Five. Ensure your big question is properly resolved, along with any subplots, plot layers and smaller questions or problems. If you're writing a series there may be things left unresolved but at least wrap them up for now. Don't literally end your book on a cliff hanger as it will leave your reader annoyed and even feeling cheated, especially if they are going to have to wait for the next instalment. Not to mention the fact that it looks like a shameless marketing tool to encourage the reader to buy the next book. That being said, it's fine – and can be very powerful – to end a series novel with a major plot twist, providing the twist reveals something pertaining to the plot of this novel as well as foreshadowing events in the next. Ending on an 'Oh my God it *was* her!' moment is much more likely to encourage your reader to buy the next instalment than a cliff hanger. Karin Slaughter's 'Criminal', mentioned above, does this brilliantly, sucker-punching the reader with the last line just as you thought Will's conflicts were – for now – resolved.

Finally, wrap up your story as soon as possible after the last big drama.

Which very nicely leads me into wrapping up this little guide. I've added an appendix looking at story-writing software, which for some writers can be incredibly useful in helping to plan and structure their story and a list of resources and recommended reading for those who want to know more, or check out some of the novels I've discussed. Reading other writers who do these things well can be inspiring and even help you develop your own style.

I'd like to leave you with one last tip that pretty much sums it all up, straight from Elmore Leonard, the author of some beautifully plotted work:

'I try to leave out the parts that people skip.'

Appendix

Story Writing Software; Does it Help?

I mentioned mind-mapping at the end of chapter one, and what a useful tool it can be for helping you plan your novel, from initial idea to tweaking your final plan. If you're more of a technical than pens and paper person there's also a software programme available (see Resources for links) that will allow you to create your mind-maps on screen. This means you can alter them at will, as well as keep them all – I often create one per chapter – in a file.

Mind-mapping software isn't the only story writing software out there either – of course mind-maps can be used for a variety of purposes, but there are programmes designed purely for novel writing. Some are free, some expensive. The question is, are they worth it?

Well, they're not going to write your novel for you, or spontaneously generate bestselling ideas. Those jobs are yours. They can however help you structure and plan your novel, and if you would prefer to work solely on your computer rather than having bits of paper strewn all over your desk, then they can be useful. Personally, I've tried a few but never kept them; I use the Review option in Microsoft Word to make notes for myself alongside the manuscript (it provides a sidebar where you can add notes at chosen points of the text and then delete them later – like electronic Post-It notes) and to track changes, and find this is all I need.

Alongside my endless bits of paper that are strewn all over the desk of course. Every writer likes to work differently, so if the idea of story-writing software appeals to you, give it a whirl. Just don't use it as yet another excuse to play around online instead of actually writing....

Story Writing Software – Pros

- Provide an easily accessible overview of your novel
- Stores all the info you need in one place
- The more complex programmes will guide you through the planning process and even provide structural templates and conflict and tension trackers

Cons

- May be difficult to use or take a long time to learn – time that could be spent writing
- Some of the tools offered are so much fun you'll never get any writing done
- The best tend to be the most expensive

I've tried and tested a few of the most popular, as well as garnering other people's opinions and reading online reviews to give you a brief overview of what's available. As to whether such programmes are useful for you, that's for you to decide. I've provided links to the programmes mentioned in the Resources section, and no doubt by the time you read this there will be updated versions available.

Power Writer

Reportedly easy and simple to use, Power Writer offers three main features – an outline feature which lets you easily navigate within your story, a composition feature, which is the word processing part where you actually write your narrative, and a whole host of story tools. The tools include character traits, research notes and a place to record all your planning and structural notes. There's also an optional feature that requires you to fill in story details before you can move on to the next part of your plan. It's great for helping you create and stick to a basic plan, ensuring your story progresses logically, and also for keeping everything you need in one place. I personally really enjoyed working with this, but found it gave me too much opportunity to procrastinate. It's also one of the more expensive, and doesn't work on Mac.

Similar programmes – MasterWriter, WriteItNow (especially recommended for in-depth characterisation)

Story Weaver

May take a while to learn how to use, but once you've got to grips with it, it can be incredibly useful, particularly for structure and plot purposes, as the emphasis is on a linear creation process which takes you through different stages from inception through to scenes, chapters and events. There are tools for both character and conflict development and there's even a feature to help you generate ideas. In short, it offers help with pretty much every-thing we've looked at in this book. Online reviews tend to rate it down as being old-fashioned and clunky compared to newer software, but if you're looking for a useful, basic structural aid, this is it. It's a lot less expensive than some others as well.

Similar programmes – MasterStoryteller

Power Structure

One of the most expensive, which is the only reason a dedicated notebook and scraps of paper person such as myself doesn't have it permanently installed on her computer. The most compre-hensive piece of software that takes a really in-depth look at structural issues that I've found so far. It even includes a planning feature based on Vogler's 12 step journey that we looked at in Chapter Two, as well as various other templates – some of which are aimed at screenwriters, as Power Structure isn't aimed at novelists but at any creative writing project, which may be a downfall if you're looking for something specific. There is a brilliant Conflict Overview feature however which allows you to plot your high and low moments and even create a graph to show tension levels. It's worth it for this feature alone. The programme, as the name indicates, does focus on structure and planning, so there are little or no features for brainstorming, research, etc. Probably the best fit for the issues covered in this book. Try using it for the 'Pulling it all Together' exercise near the end of Chapter Five.

Similar programmes – DramaticaPro

From the expensive to the free…if you're on a budget (most writers are) the two most popular freebies are

yWriter5

Created by computer programmer and writer Simon Haynes, this is a handy planning tool specifically for novelists. It helps you create a basic but changeable outline, break down your manuscript into chapters and scenes and even draw up a work schedule and keep track of your progress. I would particularly recommend this for first time novelists who are fairly new to in-depth planning.

Storybook

This is a database rather than a word-processing system that lets you store everything you need in one place, including plotlines and planning. Can be a useful structural tool, is easy to use and covers different projects – so if you've got say a novel, a short story and a memoir all on the go, you can keep everything here.

If you're not sure if story-telling software is for you, try one of the free programmes first. Other programmes also often offer free trials for a week or a month, or a limited demo that allows you to use a handful of the features, and having a play around with some of the features mentioned can help illustrate some of the points we've covered in this book. Many people learn better by practically applying their knowledge, and so trying some of these programmes may be a useful add-on to compound what you've hopefully learned so far from the previous exercises in this guide.

Remember however – none of these programmes will do the hard work for you. If you struggle with planning they can help you organise your ideas and plot more effectively, but ultimately *you* are the one writing your story.

It's in your hands now.

Go write.

Resources and Recommended Reading

Recommended works mentioned in this book

'A Casual Vacancy' – JK Rowling (Sphere, 2012)

'Banana Rose' – Natalie Goldberg (Bantam, 1997)

'Borgia Fever' – Michelle Kelly (Harlequin Historical Undone, 2014)

'Burnt Offerings' – Laurell K Hamilton (Headline, 2010)

'Cloud Atlas' – David Mitchell (Sceptre, 2004)

'Criminal' – Karin Slaughter (Cornerstone, 2012)

'Gone Girl' – Gillian Flynn (Phoenix, 2012)

'Harry Potter and the Philosophers Stone' – JK Rowling (Bloomsbury, 1997)

'How to Write' – Harry Bingham (Methuen, 2012)

'Monkeys with Typewriters' – Scarlett Thomas (Cannongate Books, 2012)

'My Sister's Keeper' – Jodi Picoult (Hodder, 2009)

'Passionate Plots' – Kelly Lawrence (Compass Books, 2014)

'Room' – Emma Donoghue (Picador, 2010)

'The Seven Basic Plots' – Christopher Booker Continuum, 2005)

'The Shining' – Stephen King (New English Library, 1986)

'Violets are Blue' – James Patterson (Headline, 2011)

'Witches Abroad' –Terry Pratchett (Corgi, 2005)

'Writing the Breakout Novel' – Donald Maass (Writer's Digest, 2002)

Other Recommended Reading

'On Writing' – Stephen King (Hodder, 2012)

'The Elements of Style'- Strunk and White (Longman, 4th ed 1999)

'The Positively Productive Writer' – Simon Whaley (Compass Books, 2012)

'The Writer's Internet' – Sarah-Beth Watkins (Compass Books, 2013)

'Writing Down the Bones' – Natalie Goldberg (Shambhala, 2005)

Story Telling Software

MindMapping – http://www.mind-mapping.co.uk

PowerStructure – http://www.powerstructure.com

PowerWriter – http://www.write-brain.com/power_writer_main.htm

StoryBook – http://storybook.en.softonic.com

StoryWeaver – http://storymind.com/storyweaver

yWriter5 – http://www.spacejock.com/yWriter5.html

Online Writer's Resources – General

Absolute Write – http://absolutewrite.com

Writer's Digest – http://www.writersdigest.com

Writers Wheel – http://www.compass-books.net

Write to Done – http://writetodone.com/

Online and Home Study Writing Courses

http://www.writersbureau.com

**COMPASS
BOOKS**

Compass Books focuses on practical and informative 'how-to' books for writers. Written by experienced authors who also have extensive experience of tutoring at the most popular creative writing workshops, the books offer an insight into the more specialised niches of the publishing game.